D0396322

No More ADHD

10 Steps To Help
Improve Your Child's Attention
And
Behavior WITHOUT Drugs!

Dr. Mary Ann Block

Block Books

Block Books are published by
The Block System, Inc.
1750 Norwood Drive
Hurst, Texas 76054

ISBN 0-96655-453-1
First Printing: May 2001
Printed in the United States of America

*This book is dedicated to
the millions of children and adults
who have been mislabeled
ADHD*

ACKNOWLEDGMENT

The extensive contributions of Joan Anderson have been invaluable in bringing this book to publication.

If Mozart or Beethoven had lived today they would have been drugged for ADHD. This would have destroyed their souls and immeasurably diminished human culture. In my opinion, the current indiscriminate drugging of children is satanic. It destroys character development and fosters a valueless culture. "When a problem arises take a drug."

In *No More ADHD*, Dr. Mary Ann Block clearly outlines reasonable solutions to the "problems" of childhood. This is a must-read for parents who are concerned about their children. Do not, and I scream *do not*, trust psychologists, psychiatrists and the current drug-pushing culture of modern education. There are superior alternatives and Dr. Mary Ann Block has a book full of them.

Julian Whitaker, M.D.

TABLE OF CONTENTS

INTRODUCTION

After writing my *No More Ritalin* book, I was surprised at how many parents called my office and made an appointment for their child before putting the information from the book in place. Even though I discussed sugar, diet, nutrients and allergies in that book, few tried any of these options before making a visit to The Block Center in the Dallas, Texas area.

Families have come to The Block Center from every state in the nation and from many countries, including Portugal, Greece, Saudi Arabia, Canada, Mexico, Bermuda and even Australia. It has been wonderful to have these families visit The Block Center and I know that I was able to help most of them.

However, many families want to try my approach at home. This is why I have written this book. It is to provide updated information in an easy-to-follow 10 Step Program for parents. I have found these steps to be the most successful in finding and treating the underlying causes of attention and behavior problems.

Before I went to medical school, I was a young mother desperately looking for answers to my child's health problem. I looked everywhere. I never stopped looking until I found the answers I needed. I read everything I could find. I understand the commitment and motivation that drives a parent to pick up and read a book like this one. It is my hope that these 10 Steps will help guide you through your journey to help improve your child's attention and behavior without drugs and with No More ADHD.

Mary Ann Block, D.O.
Medical Director, The Block Center

SO JOHNNY'S ON RITALIN®!
WHAT'S THE BIG DEAL?

By
Dr. Fred Baughman, M.D.
Reprinted with Permission from Dr. Fred Baughman

Teacher to concerned parent: Mrs. Smith, your Johnny often fidgets with his hands and feet, often leaves his seat in a classroom or in other situations where remaining seated is expected. He has difficulty playing or engaging in leisure activities quietly. He is often "on the go" and talks excessively. I'm afraid that your child will not make good grades and may even be held back. Therefore, because of his hyperactivity, I suggest you see the school psychologist for his "disease".

Perhaps he has ADD or "ADHD". You know, the mythical diseases that have never been proven and there is no foolproof testing for these so-called "disorders". Don't be concerned! Leave it up to the trained experts to know what to do. We have taken care of hundreds of children with the same symptoms. All your child needs is a schedule II drug that is in the same category as opium, cocaine, morphine, and heroin. Actually, it is an amphetamine-like drug, but in children it acts like a tranquilizer. Don't worry, Mrs. Smith, the side affects are minimal. Let's go over them now. Well, there's loss of appetite, weight loss, inability to stay asleep, heart palpitations, drowsiness, joint pain, nausea, chest pain, and abdominal pain. Sometimes this drug will stunt your child's growth. Possibly it could lower Johnny's testosterone levels and it could potentially cause Tourette's Syndrome (Tourette's in children was 1 out of 200,000 but today is 1 out of 200), or your child may just get motor tics or epileptic seizures. Oh yes, in the medical manual of mental disorders it says that this type drug can cause a persecutory delusion, paranoid state, psychosis or he may become a chemically created psychopath and he might harm himself or others. (The news media never mentioned if any of the children killing other children have been on this drug, even though there has been some evidence that this is the case). I guess they felt it wasn't important, after all, it's always the gun's fault, you know. Mrs. Smith, not to worry, more than one in every 30 American students between the ages of 5 and 19 have a prescription for this drug, according to the Drug Enforcement Administration. Production has gone from about 2000 kilograms a year one decade ago to nearly 12,000 kilograms last year. Why, even though Michigan is third in this drug's use, and that U.S. manufacturers increased the production of this drug by 62%, when asked at a Town Hall meeting, Governor Engler said he didn't know what it was! "Is that a prescription drug?" Hard to believe isn't it? Just a couple of more things Mrs. Smith, Johnny may not be able to serve his country in the armed services because of his use of this drug. Also, recent studies have shown that children who take this drug are 46% more likely to commit one felony, 36% more likely to commit two or more felonies, 25% more likely to be institutionalized in a mental facility or prison, and 15% more likely to commit suicide. (I wonder why with all the teen suicides, this drug is never mentioned!) Don't worry, Mrs. Smith, we'll have Johnny under control soon!

STEP 1—UNDERSTAND THE MEDICAL SYSTEM

As a young mother, I trusted the medical system. I thought in America we had the most advanced, scientifically sound and safe medical system in the world. People were living longer and new breakthroughs were occurring every day. I never really questioned my doctor. I just did what he recommended and trusted that my family member or I would get well if I followed his directions. But when my daughter had a health problem that put us at the mercy of conventional medicine, all my beliefs were shattered. I learned some hard lessons when Michelle was seriously ill and it changed my life forever. This is what happened.

MICHELLE'S STORY

My daughter, Michelle, had suffered with chronic bladder infections (urinary tract infections or UTI's) since age two. Various doctors treated her infections with rounds and rounds of antibiotics until she turned six at which time they began to perform invasive urological tests. Michelle's primary doctor referred her to a specialist. I informed him that right before the urinary tract infections began, we had our yard sprayed with pesticides. Michelle developed hives and swelling all over her little body. Although an antihistamine took care of the initial symptoms, I thought it might be an important piece of information since it was this exposure that marked the beginning of Michelle's chronic UTI's. I would later learn that it was a major factor. But the specialist did not think her exposure relevant and disregarded the idea without ever really considering it. Instead, he began medicating her. He gave her an antibacterial for the infections, Valium to relax the bladder and Tofranil, an anti-depressant that has the side-effect of causing urine retention, to prevent the bed-wetting. (Tofranil is also often used for ADHD symptoms.) I was baffled. The specialist had told me previously that Michelle's infections were due to her inability to release all the urine and now he was giving her a drug that caused the same effect! In addition, she only wet the bed when she had an infection. Fix the infection; the bedwetting would be resolved. I discussed this with him, but again he did not consider my information. He insisted that taking all the drugs was important and was the proper protocol for Michelle.

During this drug protocol, Michelle had one of the worst UTI's ever with severe pain and bleeding. Michelle's primary doctor, who did not realize that Michelle was on all those drugs, showed great concern and told me to go back to the specialist to immediately begin to take her off all of the drugs.

BAD ADVICE

Michelle had already been taking Valium and the antidepressant, Tofranil, for six months. When I contacted the specialist, he told me to just stop the drugs. I again questioned the approach, explaining that Michelle had experienced withdrawal symptoms whenever she missed a dose. He discarded my information as being simply a coincidence and told me that she would have no problems going off the drugs abruptly. That was bad advice. Two days later, withdrawal symptoms had consumed Michelle's every emotion and behavior. My even-tempered daughter was experiencing extreme mood swings. She was either crying her eyes out or laughing hysterically.

When I called the specialist to report Michelle's terrifying symptoms, his associate on call told me to be patient and wait it out. I didn't know then that abrupt withdrawal from Valium could be fatal. Certainly the specialist should have known this. If he did not, he should never have prescribed the drug.

I immediately called Michelle's primary doctor. He told me to put Michelle back on the drugs and gave me a slow and safer method to remove them from her system. But it was too late. Michelle's health had been compromised. The specialist had not only mismanaged her withdrawal from the drugs, but I found out later that he should have been monitoring her blood at regular intervals for any adverse reactions which are more common with long-term use of the drugs. Not only could each drug have caused my daughter serious side effects, all three together increased that risk. Michelle was sick for three years from this drug regime. She suffered with a low white blood cell count, a potential side effect of any one of the three unmonitored drugs. Low white blood cell count causes suppression of the immune system.

Michelle was very ill during that time with low-grade fevers, lymphatic swelling and continuous infections. She picked up a new bug every time we left the house so I had to keep her home and isolated for months. Doctors checked her for leukemia and a serious and sometimes life-threatening autoimmune disease called systemic lupus. I was frantic and finally relieved that Michelle did not have either of those diseases. But she was still very sick. She was put on non-stop antibiotic treatment for more than a year because it allowed her to ward off infections and to return to school. Anytime we stopped the antibiotics, she became sick again. After three years of taking Michelle from doctor to doctor and finding no help, I was extremely frustrated. Apparently, the doctors were frustrated, too. When they were not able to cure her, they decided Michelle's problem was all in her head.

TAKING CONTROL

I knew if my daughter was going to get well, I would have to find the answers myself. During my search, I found an osteopathic physician who called himself a "medical detective." I didn't know much about his profession but I decided to call him. I told him that I would be in charge of my daughter's care and that he would have to listen to me because I knew my daughter best. He told me he wouldn't have it any other way. That moment marked the beginning of the road back to good health for Michelle. This doctor explained that osteopathic medicine centers on the belief that the body, given the proper tools, can heal itself. Not only was this approach refreshing, it gave me the first glimmer of hope I had felt since Michelle's ordeal began. This osteopathic physician offered me options and support rather than another prescription. He looked for the underlying causes of Michelle's health problems, respected my input, and shared his information with me.

NEVER AGAIN

This doctor showed me a new and more rational way to practice medicine. I was optimistic about this approach. I wanted so much to regain my confidence in medicine, but I was still afraid and guarded. I felt that I needed to know what doctors know in order to protect my family. I decided to become an osteopathic physician. So at the age of 39, out of self-defense and for the sole purpose of protecting my family, I entered osteopathic medical school.

THE DRUG COMPANY'S INFLUENCE
ON MEDICAL EDUCATION

While in medical school I discovered what I believe to be the problem with medicine. Although first year medical students learn about the physiology of how the body works, the real learning emphasis for the rest of their training is on naming a disease and prescribing a drug. It is no wonder that Michelle's flawed treatment was based solely on the use of medications. When medical students begin their courses, the PhDs in the basic sciences who teach them in the medical school are also doing research at the institution. There is a saying in academia, "Publish or perish." This means that professors want to write articles for their professional journals in order to secure their positions at the school and advance professionally.

In the sciences, the PhD must conduct studies and write about their findings in order to succeed professionally. These studies are funded with grants and other outside money, which brings funds into the medical school. Medical schools build prestige and benefit financially when faculty members are awarded numerous grants. Since most research is based on drug studies, it should not surprise us that the pharmaceutical industry is a top contributor for underwriting these studies. When medical students move into rotations and residency programs, it is common to find that many of the doctors who train them are also involved in drug studies and receiving funds from the pharmaceutical industry. When the focus of the medical school's basic science and clinical faculty is on drugs, the medical training will also focus on drugs.

THE DRUG COMPANY'S INFLUENCES ON DOCTORS

The drug companies are also a strong influence on doctors after medical school. The drug companies send representatives to doctor's offices and bring a multitude of specialty items with the company's name on them. They give away pads and pens and if a physician is really good at prescribing their drug, according to one representative I know, a company might send the doctor on a trip to Hawaii. This is a very common practice and it provides a great deal of motivation to use that company's product. When doctors go to continuing medical education courses (a certain number of hours are required each year in order to maintain a medical license), the doctors who speak to the groups are often paid by pharmaceutical companies to talk about that company's newest drug. Many of these doctors are also conducting research funded by the company.

DRUG STUDIES AND FRAUD

A recent *60 Minutes* show reported that doctors receive between $50,000 and $250,000 per study and may be involved in as many as 30 to 40 studies at one time. The report focused on one physician who had falsified his research data, then published articles in the medical journals about his findings. It was noted that this occurs often but there is no way to know how often unless someone on the inside comes forward and exposes the fraudulent behavior. These are the people who are teaching our next generation of physicians. We have physicians and PhDs who are focusing on drugs, and receiving funding from the pharmaceutical industry. With this dubious relationship between doctors and the drug companies, how can the unsuspecting public trust a drug to be safe and effective?

FDA DRUG ADVISERS HAVE FINANCIAL CONFLICT OF INTEREST

According to articles in both *Reuters News* and *USA Today*, 54 percent of the experts that the FDA consults on medicines to be approved had a direct financial interest in the drugs or topics they were evaluating. These financial conflicts of interest include stock ownership, consulting fees, or research grants.

Even though federal law prohibits the FDA from using experts with financial conflicts of interest, the FDA waived the restriction more than 800 times since 1998. Since 1992 the FDA has kept the details of any conflict secret so it is not possible to determine the amount of money or the identity of drug companies involved.

The *USA Today* article stated, "These pharmaceutical experts, about 300 (experts) on 18 advisory committees, make decisions that affect the health of millions of Americans and billions of dollars in drug sales. With few exceptions, the FDA follows the committees' advice."

ADHD MARKETING

The establishment of a non-profit, parents' group to advocate a drug would be a brilliant marketing strategy for any drug company. A parents' group could make claims and promote the use of drugs much more effectively than the drug company and without the same restrictions companies face from FDA and FTC regulations. *The Merrow Report*, a news program on PBS, reported that the manufacturer of Ritalin®, Ciba Geigy (now Novartis) gave almost $1 million to the support group Children and Adults with Attention Deficit Disorder (CHADD) between 1991 and 1994. This group advocates the use of psychiatric drugs for children. This relationship between the drug company and a non-profit parents' group poses another potential financial conflict of interest that should be a source of concern for parents. In a document resulting from a year-long probe into CHADD's finances, the U.S. Drug Enforcement Agency (DEA) warned that the contributions are "not well-known by the public, including CHADD members that have relied upon CHADD for guidance."

In a *Washington Post* report, February 5, 1996, Gene Haislip, DEA division control head stated, "A lot of people don't know Ritalin® is like cocaine. It can be very dangerous and must be treated with respect." He called the relationship between the manufacturer and CHADD an "unhealthy co-mingling of medical and commercial interests."

CHADD says it does not promote use of Ritalin® but does mention it in the context of treatment options. However, CHADD's actions do not appear to be so neutral. In 1995, CHADD tried to persuade the DEA to classify Ritalin® as a Schedule III drug, which would have made it easier to obtain.

Step 1—Understand the Medical System

IF ALL YOU HAVE IS A HAMMER . . .

So it really is all about drugs. That's what medicine is about. I now know how naïve I was to think that when I took my daughter to doctors, they would have all the answers and know how to help her be well. In actuality what they knew how to do very well was prescribe drugs. What is taught in medical school is how to name symptoms with a disease or a syndrome, and then write a prescription to drug it. There is a saying, "If all you have is a hammer, then everything looks like a nail." Well, that's what's happening in medicine -- If all you have is a prescription pad, then everyone gets a drug.

DRUGS COVER UP SYMPTOMS

It may surprise you to learn that drugs rarely cure anything. Drugs can cover up symptoms while the body heals itself and that is often how it works. I am not saying that all drugs are bad and that we shouldn't use drugs, but I do think it's important for the public to understand that a doctor's training emphasizes, almost exclusively, the use of drugs. Sometimes this use is appropriate, but it is always important to understand the limits and risks of using drugs. I learned the hard way. Let's look at how this focus on drugs may affect an ADHD label that a child might be given.

GOING BY THE BOOK

Attention Deficit Hyperactivity Disorder (ADHD) is officially a psychiatric label. When children are diagnosed with ADHD, they are considered to have a psychiatric disorder. In 1987, ADHD was literally voted into existence by the American Psychiatric Association and inserted into the Diagnostic and Statistical Manual of Mental Disorders (DSM). The DSM is psychiatry's "billing bible" for diagnosing and assigning insurance-payment codes. The DSM lists psychiatric disorders and the symptoms used to describe the so-called disorders. Psychiatrists write the book and decide what behaviors or groups of behaviors are psychiatric disorders.

A group of psychiatrists get together every few years and sit down in a room and talk about various groups of behaviors that they think should be considered psychiatric disorders. Then they vote to include certain groups of behaviors as psychiatric disorders in the next edition of the book with a list of symptoms. Through a simple vote, with no objective means to define this psychiatric label, a new disorder is born and begins to take on a life of its own. Within one year of deciding to insert ADHD in the DSM, 500,000 children in the United States were diagnosed with the disorder and today the number is closer to 5 million. A common denominator of these psychiatric disorders is that there is no objective way to define or to diagnose them. If you have high blood pressure, your doctor can objectively measure and diagnose the problem. If you have diabetes, your doctor can objectively measure your blood sugar and give you a diagnosis. There is no way to measure for a psychiatric diagnosis.

The signs and symptoms of ADHD listed in *The Diagnostic and Statistical Manual* (DSM IV) are completely subjective. *[See Figure 1]*

Actually I find that many of us possess these behaviors. I prefer to stand up and give a lecture rather than sit in the audience because I can't sit still for an hour at a time.

Step 1—Understand the Medical System

Figure 1

Attention Deficit Hyperactivity Disorder

A. Inattention: Six (or more) of the following symptoms of inattention have persisted for at least 6 months to a degree that is maladaptive and inconsistent with developmental level:

(a) often fails to give close attention to details or makes careless mistakes in schoolwork, work or other activities
(b) often has difficulty sustaining attention in tasks or play activities
(c) often does not seem to listen when spoken to directly
(d) often does not follow through on instructions and fails to finish schoolwork, chores or duties in the workplace (not due to oppositional behavior or failure to understand instructions)
(e) often has difficulty organizing tasks and activities
(f) often avoids, dislikes or is reluctant to engage in tasks that require sustained mental effort (such as schoolwork or homework)
(g) often loses things necessary for tasks or activities (e.g., toys, school assignments, pencils books or tools)
(h) is often easily distracted by extraneous stimuli
(i) is often forgetful in daily activities

If you have six of these 12 subjective symptoms, you get the diagnosis. Ask yourself how many of these symptoms you possess-probably quite a few. That's because these are normal behavior traits. No one enjoys spending a lot of time on activities they do not like. Certainly not six-year-old children. Now lets look at the list for hyperactivity/impulsivity.

B. Hyperactivity/Impulsivity: Six (or more) of the following symptoms of hyperactivity-impulsivity have persisted for at least 6 months to a degree that is maladaptive and inconsistent with developmental level:
Hyperactivity
(a) often fidgets with hands or feet or squirms in seat

Figure 1—cont'd.

(b) often leaves seat in classroom or in other situations in which remaining in seat is expected
(c) often runs about or climbs excessively in situations in which it is inappropriate (in adolescents or adults, may be limited to subjective feelings of restlessness)
(d) often has difficulty playing or engaging in leisure activities quietly
(e) is often "on the go" or often acts as if "driven by a motor"
(f) often talks excessively
Impulsivity
(g) often blurts out answers before questions have been completed
(h) often has difficulty awaiting turn
(i) often interrupts or intrudes on others (e.g., butts into conversations or games)

C. Some hyperactive-impulsive or inattentive symptoms that caused impairment were present before age 7 years.

D. Some impairment from the symptoms is present in two or more settings (e.g., school or work and at home)

E. There must be clear evidence of clinically significant impairment in social, academic or occupational functioning.

F. The symptoms do not occur exclusively during the course of a Pervasive Developmental Disorder, Schizophrenia or other Psychotic Disorder and are not better accounted for by another mental disorder (e.g., Mood Disorder, Anxiety Disorder, Disassociative Disorder or a Personality Disorder).

Some might say then that I am ADHD. But I think my behavior is normal and it certainly has not interfered with my productivity. And I am not taking Ritalin®. This is just another example of the subjective nature of the ADHD diagnosis.

One therapist or teacher may see a child and think that he or she is fidgeting or blurting out answers while another therapist or teacher sees a perfectly normal, bright child who knows the answer and is excited to get it out. The diagnosis of ADHD is not consistent from one person to another and the subjectivity of this diagnosis is a large part of the problem.

CONCERNS ABOUT THE ADHD DIAGNOSIS AND TREATMENT

In 1998, the National Institutes of Health convened a three-day conference on ADHD and the treatments used for it. Many leading experts from across the U.S. came to present their data to the panel yet failed to provide any scientific evidence to validate ADHD as a neurobiologic brain disorder. Parents are being told there is something wrong with their child's brain, yet no one can prove it. Then their child is labeled "mentally ill" with a diagnosis of "ADHD," a disorder that came into being, not by science, but by a majority vote. Their child is then subjected to mind-altering drugs in order to change the child's behavior. This scenario is occurring because physicians use the DSM book with its subjective descriptions of disorders as a guide to diagnose their patients with psychiatric problems.

Many doctors just take the teacher's word on it. If the teacher thinks a child has ADHD and informs the doctor, the doctor writes a prescription for Ritalin® or Adderall or some other psychiatric drug. Often the doctor will label the child ADHD and prescribe a psychiatric drug solely on the teacher's word, without ever doing a physical exam or looking for any treatable medical or educational problems. Under this system it is easy to be diagnosed with a psychiatric disorder.

THE MEDICAL SYSTEM AND ADHD

When I was a guest on *The Montel Williams Show*, there was also a psychiatrist on the show. The psychiatrist was supporting the use of drugs for ADHD and I was discussing the fact that there are many underlying health problems that can cause the same symptoms. On the show, I mentioned that I rarely see a child who has had a physical exam, much less lab work, before being diagnosed with ADHD and prescribed mind altering drugs. And then, on national television, the psychiatrist said, "Look, we're psychiatrists. It's a psychiatric diagnosis. Psychiatric diagnoses are based on the history. Psychiatrists don't do physical exams."

I know from experience that many doctors don't do physicals exams before prescribing psychiatric drugs so I was glad that this psychiatrist shared this with all who were watching that day. My clinical experience confirms that this is usually what occurs to children who are diagnosed with ADHD. They see a doctor, but the doctor does not do a physical exam or look for any health or learning problems before giving the child an ADHD diagnosis and a prescription drug. This is not how I was taught to practice medicine. In my medical education, I was taught to do a complete history and physical exam. I was taught to consider something called a "differential diagnosis." To do this, one must consider all possible underlying causes of the symptoms.

After that the physician comes up with a list of the possible reasons for the symptoms. In order to determine which on the list is the real cause of the symptoms, the doctor must then do any lab work or other tests, which can confirm or eliminate each one. Until this process is complete the actual diagnosis is just a guess. Once the cause is discovered, the next step is to treat it.

I prefer to determine if there is a natural way, or some life-style change that can be used whenever possible. But I always tell my patients all their options. This is called informed consent which means that the physician has explained to the patient all of the different options available and the potential risks or side effects of each. If this doctor-patient interaction sounds as if it would take a lot of time, you are right. It does take time. That is why I spend as much as an hour with a new patient. To me this is how medicine should be practiced. It is how I was taught to practice in medical school. Even psychiatrists went to medical school and were taught how to do physical exams.

STUPID OR LYING

In my opinion, if a child has been diagnosed and treated without a complete history and physical and if a child has been prescribed a drug without informed consent, then that child has not been adequately evaluated or treated. Once, while at a conference in New Jersey where I spoke on ADHD, I was on a panel with a prominent and well know physician. Someone in the audience asked this physician if what he said was correct, why her child's doctor disagreed with him. The speaker responded, "Your child's doctor is either stupid or he's lying." A more gentle way of expressing this might be to say that the child's doctor was uninformed or giving out inaccurate information. Her child's doctor told this woman that her child had ADHD and the drug that he was prescribing was perfectly safe. As that statement can be demonstrated to be false, the doctor must have been uninformed or misinforming.

DRUG RISKS

No drug is perfectly safe. At a certain dose all drugs can be toxic and dangerous. Knowing which dose will not do harm is the tricky part. I have heard doctors say that when given in the proper dose, Ritalin® is perfectly safe. The National Institutes of Health (NIH) has stated that there is no valid way to actually diagnose ADHD. I see no way for anyone to actually come up with the proper dose of a drug to treat a disorder whose existence cannot be objectively determined. In addition, the NIH report further revealed that most of the drugs used to treat ADHD symptoms were only studied for a few months. We cannot possibly know the long-term side effects for drugs that were not tested long term. I would not want my child to be taking a drug for several years that had been tested only three months.

LONG-TERM DRUG USE

I have heard many physicians state that "Ritalin® has been used for years and we know more about it than any other drug." Ritalin® has been used since the 1950's so many doctors believe that over that extent of time the drug has proven itself safe for use in children. In the past, however, the drug was prescribed for short periods of time until it was judged that the child had outgrown the symptoms of hyperactivity and inattentiveness. Now we know that children do not outgrow the symptoms but continue to have them for life unless something is done to eliminate the underlying cause.

So, while Ritalin® has been used for years, it was not used on the same child for years until fairly recently. Today children and adults are taking Ritalin® for ten to twenty years. The cumulative effects a drug has on the body when taken for that many years are very different than when it is used for only a year or two.

I believe we've already had many warnings about problems with the long-term use of psychiatric drugs. The most tragic example was that of the 14-year-old in Pontiac, Michigan who died of a heart attack. The medical examiner reported that his death was a result of taking Ritalin® for ten years.

KIDDIE COCAINE

Would you put your children on cocaine to make them sit still, pay attention and behave? Of course not. But some of you may have done exactly that without even knowing it! The drug in question is Ritalin® which is pharmacologically similar to cocaine. They each go to the same receptor sites in the brain. Ritalin® and cocaine are used interchangeably in scientific studies. The DEA has reported this and also states that Ritalin® produces cocaine-like effects.

The DEA says that taking Ritalin® predisposes takers to cocaine's reinforcing effect— a very benign way to say addiction. According to DEA Congressional testimony, "neither animals nor humans can tell the difference between cocaine, amphetamines or methylphenidate (Ritalin®), when they are administered the same way in comparable doses. In short, they produce effects that are nearly identical." [See the DEA Report, *Figure 2*.]

AND MORE DRUGS

In addition to the most commonly prescribed drug, Ritalin®, other drugs used for ADHD symptoms include Adderall, Dexedrine and Cylert, which are amphetamines or "speed" type drugs. Amphetamines are controlled substances because they have a high likelihood of abuse. Cylert can cause liver damage. Adderall and Dexadrine are straight amphetamines. Surely there is not a "proper" dose of amphetamines that can safely be prescribed to a child. Tofranil and Norpramine, which are also used for ADHD, are tricyclic antidepressants. The literature on Norpramine comes with a warning to alert physicians that Norpramine can cause sudden cardiac death in children. There are many other side effects to the drugs prescribed for ADHD symptoms. I recommend to all my patients that they get a drug insert from the pharmacist or purchase a *Physician's Desk Reference* (PDR) for themselves.

The PDR is a very thick book, which has detailed information about each drug and the same information listed in the drug insert. While most prescription drugs have potential side effects, we don't know in advance who will actually suffer from these problems. Everyone should weigh the potential side effects against their actual symptoms. If the side effects sound worse than the problem, they might not choose to take the drug. The reason the PDR lists side effects is because they can and do occur. Everyone should decide individually if the benefit of taking the drug is

Step 1—Understand the Medical System

Figure 2

U.S. Department of Justice Drug Enforcement Agency (DEA)
Drug and Chemical Evaluation Section,1995

Methylphenidate (Ritalin®) - Overview

1. Ritalin® is a Schedule II stimulate, structurally and phar-
    macologically similar to amphetamines and cocaine and
    has the same dependency profile of cocaine and other
    stimulants.

2. Ritalin® produces amphetamine and cocaine-like reinforc-
    ing effects including increased rate of euphoria and drug lik-
    ing. Treatment with Ritalin® in childhood predisposes takers
    to cocaine's reinforcing effects.

3. In humans, chronic administration of Ritalin® produced tol-
    erance and showed cross-tolerance with cocaine and am-
    phetamines.

4. Ritalin® is chosen over cocaine in self-administered prefer-
    ence studies in non-human primates.

5. Ritalin® produces behavioral, physiological and reinforcing
    effects similar to amphetamines.

6. Ritalin® substitutes for cocaine and amphetamines in
    scientific studies.

7. Children medicated with Ritalin® who tried cocaine reported
    higher levels of drug dependence than those who had not
    used Ritalin®.

8. Ritalin® abuse is neither benign or rare in occurrence and is
    accurately described as producing severe dependence. Swe-
    den removed Ritalin® from its market in 1968 because of
    widespread abuse.

Figure 2—cont'd.

9. More high school seniors were abusing Ritalin® than those taking it medically prescribed.

Side-effects of Ritalin®: increased blood pressure, heart rate, respirations and temperature; appetite suppression, weight loss, growth retardation; facial tics, muscle twitching, central nervous system stimulation, euphoria, nervousness, irritability and agitation, psychotic episodes, violent behavior, paranoid delusions, hallucinations, bizarre behaviors, heart arrhythmias, palpitations and high blood pressure; tolerance and psychological dependence and death

10. Ritalin® will affect normal children and adults the same as those with attention and behavior problems. Effectiveness of Ritalin® is not diagnostic.

CHADD, non-profit organization, which promotes the use of Ritalin®, also receives a great deal of money from the drug manufacturer of Ritalin®. CHADD does not inform its members of the abuse problems of Ritalin®. CHADD portrays the drug as a benign, mild stimulant that is not associated with abuse of serious side-effects. Statements by CHADD are inconsistent with scientific literature.

11. The International Narcotics Control Board expressed concern that CHADD is actively lobbying for the use of Ritalin® in children.

12. Ritalin® is one of the top ten drugs involved in drug thefts and is being abused by health professionals as well as street addicts.

Note from Dr. Block: Since Adderall and Dexadrine are amphetamines, the above statements would also be true of them.

worth the risk of the potential side effect.

Another drug prescribed for children is Clonidine or Catapres, which is an adult high blood pressure medication. This "adult" drug has never been tested on children under the age of 18 and is not indicated for use for anyone under age 18. What often happens is that the drugs are given to an adult and the adult reports being better able to focus and to sit still. Then doctors decide to use these drugs on younger and younger children until they get down to the two- to four-year-old age groups. So even though there are no studies conducted on children and no determination of its safety for children, even in the short term, the drugs are prescribed to children for the long term.

"OFF LABEL" DRUG USE

It is perfectly legal for doctors to prescribe drugs that have not been tested on the age group or for the purpose for which they are prescribed. This is called "off label use" and it occurs all the time. I find it quite interesting that when a drug called, Secretin was found to help some children with autism many doctors said it should not be used for this purpose. Giving the drug to autistic children was certainly an "off label use." Its positive effects on these children were found quite by accident.

I have many patients who have been labeled autistic. Many of their parents had inquired about Secretin and been lectured to by a neurologist, psychiatrist or pediatrician who said the drug had not been tested on children nor had it been approved for use with autistic symptoms. The doctors were adamant that the parents should not use this drug on their children. Ironically, these same doctors had been prescribing psychiatric drugs that had not been tested on children and which had potentially severe side effects to the very children whose parents they were cautioning against Secretin. Yet, the adverse reactions to Secretin, as listed by the drug manufacturer in the PDR, are as follows: "No adverse reactions to Secretin-Ferring have been reported." I wonder why these doctors can so readily prescribe psychiatric drugs with many dangerous potential side effects, yet deny a child an opportunity to use a drug with no known side effects, particularly when both drugs are "off label use?" It makes no sense to me.

ANTIDEPRESSANT DRUGS

There are approximately ten different Selective Seritonin Reuptake Inhibitor (SSRI) drugs such as Prozac, Paxil, Luvox, and Zoloft also commonly prescribed for ADHD symptoms. These drugs come with a host of potential side effects and are not indicated for children under the age of 18. According to the FDA's *Adverse Drug Reaction Report on Prozac, 1988-1992,* more than 90 children and adolescents suffered suicidal or violent self-destructive behaviors while taking Prozac.

According to the drug companies manufacturing these psychiatric drugs, every one can cause heart problems and paranoia. It does not mean that everyone will have heart problems or paranoia, but if it is your child who gets the side effect, for you that's 100%. Remember when deciding whether or not to take a prescription drug, informed consent should be included in the decision process. If your doctor does not tell you the potential side effects, you should educate yourself by asking your pharmacist for the drug insert.

Step 1—Understand the Medical System

When you pick up a prescription, many pharmacies will give you some information about the drug, including side effects. This list is usually just the most common or most likely side effects. Some of the more serious adverse reactions may not be the most common. If the side effect happens to you or to your child, it doesn't really matter that only a small percentage were expected to experience it.

ONLY IN AMERICA

The United Nations Controlled Substance Board (UNCSB) reported stable use of methylphenidate or Ritalin® from the years 1985 to 1992. In 1992 sales of Ritalin® shot up and between 1992 and 1996 the use tripled. The UNCB has a great deal of concern about the increased Ritalin® prescriptions because the United States consumes 90% of the world's Ritalin®. In some countries, Ritalin® is not even available.

I see patients who come to my office from all over the world. When they come from other countries with a child labeled with ADHD and are being pressured to put their child on Ritalin®, I have noticed that there is always an American connection. For instance, one child I saw from Saudi Arabia was in an American school there and the school was insistent that he be on Ritalin®. When the parents moved their child to a British school they said their child had no more problems.

DRUG ABUSE CLIMBS WITH RITALIN USE

I find it interesting and disturbing that during this four year period when Ritalin® use spiked, overall drug use among teenagers rose 105% with cocaine use up 166%. This correlation is interesting because of the similarity of

Step 1—Understand the Medical System

Ritalin® and cocaine in effecting the same receptor sites in the brain and triggering the same effect on the body when taken in the same manner.

In medical research the two drugs are used interchangeably. Ritalin® blocks cocaine uptake and cocaine blocks Ritalin® uptake. So scientists who conduct cocaine research use Ritalin® to help them identify certain areas of the brain. Children taking Ritalin® have figured this out, sometimes crushing their pills and snorting the powder just like cocaine. Ritalin® is being sold and used by teenagers and college students as a street drug.

These students have told me how easy and how cheap it is to get a prescription of Ritalin®. They just tell their doctor they are having trouble concentrating and paying attention in class and they are handed a prescription of a Class II controlled substance that they can now snort and sell or give to their friends. One college student told me she had been taking Ritalin® since high school and that she was unable to stop taking it. She felt she was addicted and had no trouble getting more prescriptions from her doctor. If a health insurance plan covers prescription drugs, these kids can get this Class II Controlled Substance for the cost of a co-pay.

SUBJECTIVE DIAGNOSIS

When the NIH held a special conference concerning the diagnosis and treatment of ADHD in 1998, they issued a summary of their findings. This is what they said followed by my commentary:

1. There is no independent, valid test to diagnose ADHD.

This means to me there is no objective measurement for diagnosing ADHD. You can't draw blood and find it. You can't perform a CT scan and see it. There is nothing that you can objectively find to prove a diagnosis of ADHD. The diagnosis is often made with the Connors Rating Scale or some other subjective method, which the parents and teachers fill out. It is simply asking someone's opinion. So the diagnosis is subjective, determined by the biases and perspective of the person making the decision. If that person is someone who believes that children should sit still and be quiet then the child will probably get the ADHD diagnosis. However, if the person thinks children should be allowed to move around and fidget, then the child will be thought normal. Yet parents around the country are paying large sums of money to have their children tested for ADHD even though there is no valid test for it. Once a child is labeled with ADHD, the child is usually prescribed a drug, which can carry many risks. These drugs are prescribed to treat a diagnosis that does not really exist.

2. There is no data to prove that ADHD is a result of a brain dysfunction.

There are no studies. That's the problem with psychiatric diagnoses. The psychiatrist does not do any testing. The psychiatrist listens to the history and then prescribes a drug. This is very puzzling to me because these psychiatrists went to medical school just like I did and they should have learned how to do physical exams and a "differential diagnosis." To do a differential diagnosis, a doctor should do a physical exam, lab work, allergy testing and diet evaluations. The doctor should do everything possible to determine the reason for the symptoms.

Step 1—Understand the Medical System

The doctor should not just listen to the history and give a psychiatric diagnosis and a drug. After the differential diagnosis and before treatment the doctor should then provide the patient or parent with "informed consent."

3. Most randomized clinical trials of drugs are very short, up to three months.

The Federal Drug Administration (FDA) recognizes the limits of this kind of testing because the agency has said that a drug may be prescribed to the public for 10-20 years before we understand the complete potential side effects of these drugs. Some have even suggested that we avoid the use of drugs until they have been on the market for 2-3 years.

4. There is actually no information on the long-term outcome of drug treatment.

There are no studies looking at the results of using these drugs for years and years. Even though this information is not available, I see children who have been prescribed these drugs for 10 years or longer.

5. Stimulants do not normalize the entire range of behaviors.

Even if the drugs do help some, it has been found that the drugs show little improvement in academic achievement or social skills. It may appear to help initially, but the studies show that it does not improve academic achievement over time. Some parents and teachers are surprised at this, but this was the published finding. Just because someone is quieter and can sit still longer does not necessarily equate with improved learning.

6. There is no data on the inattentive type of ADHD.

So for all of those children I have seen in my office who have been labeled with Attention Deficit Disorder (ADD) (Inattentive type) and put on a psychiatric drug, there is no data indicating this is appropriate. There is no data showing the efficacy of drug treatment for adolescents and adults either. Yet thousands of teens and adults are prescribed drugs each year for ADHD symptoms.

7. The drugs (used for ADHD) can cause compulsive and mood disorders and drug availability can lead to illicit drug abuse.

If there is no valid test for ADHD, no data proving ADHD is a brain dysfunction, no long-term studies of the drugs effects, and if the drugs do not improve academic performance or social skills and the drugs can cause compulsive and mood disorders and can lead to illicit drug use, why in the world are millions of children, teenagers and adults in this country being labeled ADHD and prescribed these drugs?

PSYCHIATRIC DRUGS: STATISTICALLY LOW BENEFITS

In my experience, Ritalin® does not cure ADHD symptoms. We used to think that children outgrew their symptoms, but we now know that this is not the case. Even if a drug is helpful, when the drug is stopped, the symptoms return. A long-term study reported in the *Journal of the American Academy of Child and Adolescent Psychiatry* followed a group of hyperactive children over an eight-year period. At the end of the study, 80% continued to

---

Figure 3

1998 National Institute of Health Conference on ADHD
Report Summary

- No valid, independent, consistent test available
- No data indicating it is a brain dysfunction
- Drugs don't normalize all behaviors
- Kids on drugs still have higher level of behavior problems
- Kids on drugs show little improvement in academic and social skills
- No information on treatment for more than one year
- High doses of drugs cause hypertension, nervous and cardiovascular systems damage

---

have the ADHD diagnosis and continued to have the symptoms. What is even more alarming is that another 60% of these children progressed to more serious diagnoses, Oppositional-Defiant Disorder and Conduct Disorder. While these are also psychiatric labels, their symptoms are more severe. So not only did the drugs not work for 80% of the children, but more than 60% of the children actually got worse while taking them.

Adding other treatments along with the drugs did not appear to make any difference. More than 80% of the children in the study had been medicated. More than 63% of the children had the use of mental health services and more than 35% had the use of special educational services. The results showed that relying predominately on medication, even while using other services, yielded at best a 20% success rate with a 60% chance of worsening of symptoms. That doesn't speak well for the benefits of drug treatment.

NEGATIVE EFFECTS OF RITALIN®

The short-term side effects of Ritalin® and other amphetamine type drugs are well known and occur frequently. They are appetite loss, insomnia, weight loss, headaches, irritability, sudden mood changes, growth suppression and exacerbation of tics. In my experience, I find that doctors who prescribe Ritalin® are very comfortable with these symptoms. My patients report to me that the prescribing doctor finds them acceptable. Actually, many of these symptoms should not be considered side effects, as they are common and simply the usual, expected effects of the drug. These are the same effects that occur when someone takes "speed."

RISKS AND SIDE EFFECTS

Long-term use of the drugs used to treat the symptoms of ADHD may be dangerous. We should be very concerned about the effects that these drugs can have on the heart and on the vascular system as well as on the kidneys and other organs. According to the NIH, the clinical trials for the drugs were no more then three months long, yet we are putting children on these drugs for years without valid information on the long term consequences. The children are like little lab animals and are themselves currently testing the safety and efficacy of the long-term use of these drugs without even knowing it.

RITALIN® IS <u>NOT</u> ESSENTIAL TO LIFE

While trying to convince a parent to put a child on Ritalin® or other psychiatric drugs, parents have told me that a doctor, teacher or friend has said to them, "If your child had diabetes, you would give them insulin. Giving a child Ritalin® for ADHD is the same thing." Let me clear this up right now. ADHD is not like diabetes and Ritalin® is not like insulin. Diabetes is a real medical condition that can be objectively diagnosed. ADHD is an invented label with no objective, valid means of identification. Insulin is a natural hormone produced by the body and it is essential for life. Ritalin® is a chemically-derived amphetamine-like drug that is not necessary for life. Diabetes is an insulin deficiency. Attention and behavioral problems are not a Ritalin® deficiency.

STREET DRUG EFFECTS

Additionally, the psychiatrist's *Diagnostic and Statistical Manual* (DSM) cites two other interesting diagnoses, each with an equally interesting list of symptoms, Amphetamine Dependency Abuse and Amphetamine Intoxication. Ritalin® and many other drugs used to treat ADHD are amphetamines or are amphetamine-like. According to the DSM, symptoms of amphetamine dependency include depression, irritability and social isolation. Amphetamine Intoxication can cause euphoria, restlessness, anxiety, tension, repetitive behaviors, anger, fighting, impaired judgment as well as chest pain, heart arrhythmias, confusion, seizures, coma and impaired social and occupational functioning. Yet, these drugs which can cause terrible symptoms and are illegally abused and sold on the streets, are being prescribed to children, some as young as two years old. How can these drugs possibly be safe for young children?

I continue to be shocked that doctors can so thoughtlessly prescribe Ritalin® and other amphetamine-like drugs to children when they know the potential problems. The psychiatrist's own book, the DSM, describes the potential problems of the abuse of drugs like Ritalin® and Adderall. In addition, the DSM explains that the symptoms of cocaine abuse and dependency are the same as amphetamine abuse and dependency and that experienced users cannot tell the difference between amphetamines and cocaine. Although their own guidebook is clear and definitive on the negative effects of these drugs, psychiatrists and other doctors continue to prescribe these drugs to young children.

Perhaps the doctors prescribing these drugs are unaware of the possible serious side effects. According to a report by the FDA, less than one percent of doctors read the labels and know the side-effects of the drugs they are prescribing. Now, that's a scary thought! Expressing great concern, the FDA is trying to develop a method to make it easier for doctors to read about the adverse effects of the drugs they prescribe. All a doctor has to do is open up the PDR and read about the drug! How difficult is that? Since many doctors learn about the drugs they prescribe exclusively from the pharmaceutical company manufacturing the substance, the doctor may never learn about the side effects. Unless the doctor asks, the drug company representative, who wants the doctor to write the prescription, is unlikely to offer the information. One drug company representative told me that I'm the only physician he calls on who asks him about side effects.

BABIES ON RITALIN®

According to an article in *The Journal of the American Medical Association*, between 1991 and 1995, the use of Ritalin,® Prozac and other psychiatric drugs increased two to threefold in two- to four- year olds. This is interest-

ing since the makers of Ritalin® say that safety and efficacy has not been established for anyone less than 6 years
of age and 18 for Prozac.

DRUG DEATHS

In Pontiac, Michigan the medical examiner reported that
the 10-year use of Ritalin® which was prescribed to treat a
young man for hyperactivity led to his fatal heart attack at
age 14. The medical examiner reported that the changes
in the child's heart were a result of long-term Ritalin®
use. The parents said that they were pressured to put their
child on Ritalin® because the school threatened to report
them to Child Protective Services for medical negligence if
they did not. So the parents reluctantly put their child on
the drug which the medical examiner says ultimately
killed him.

The psychiatric community expressed outrage at the
medical examiner for his findings. They disputed the report, saying that Ritalin® has been used for 40 years and
claiming the drug to be safe and its side effects harmless.
But this is an erroneous argument because we have not
used Ritalin® for years in the same patients. Long-term
use is a new phenomenon. Even the drug manufacturer
states that Ritalin® can have adverse effects on the heart.

As pharmacologically similar to cocaine and indistin-
guishable from that drug to experienced users, Ritalin®
creates an interesting paradox. Can you imagine schools
pressuring parents to put their children on cocaine and
doctors approving and supporting its use? If the Michigan
boy had been taking cocaine for ten years rather than a
legally-prescribed drug and then died of a heart attack,
the community would have been stunned and outraged.
They would have hunted down the drug-pushers and

started a drug-prevention and awareness program to protect other children. But because the drug in question was Ritalin®, the doctors angrily protested the medical examiner's conclusion that Ritalin® affected the boy's heart and ultimately killed him.

PRESCRIPTION DRUGS AND VIOLENCE

According to national news reports in January 1999, ten days after Ryan Ehlis, a college student in Bismark, North Dakota, began taking Adderall to control his attention deficit disorder and to help him with his college studies, he slipped into a psychotic fog and killed his infant daughter. He said God told him to do it. The courts found him innocent after testimony by a psychiatrist and by the manufacturer of the drug that the "psychotic state" was a very rare side effect of Adderall use.

The drug's labeling does warn that, in rare circumstances, it can cause psychotic episodes, even at recommended doses. How do we know who will be affected in this manner? How many people who were prescribed Adderall were told of this possible side effect? It is important to note that every drug prescribed for the symptoms called ADHD can cause either paranoia or psychotic behaviors and heart problems according to their manufacturers.

When I was in Arizona presenting a seminar on ADHD, a woman approached me after my talk and said she experienced a similar side effect from Adderall. While driving she suffered a psychotic episode and her child was killed. This kind of thing may be happening all over the country and we can't predict when or where or to whom it will happen next. That has also been my concern about the violence in our schools.

Step 1—Understand the Medical System

SCHOOL VIOLENCE

There is an alarming trend of student violence and mass shootings in schools today. I have been traveling to various states testifying at legislative hearings on the connection between school violence and psychiatric drugs. There appears to be more than a coincidental connection. Eric Harris from Littleton, Colorado was on Luvox when he shot up Columbine High School. If you read the drug insert from the pharmacutical company that makes Luvox and see the symptoms it can cause, it should not be a surprise that he was involved in such a violent act.

According to the manufacturer Luvox can cause: mania, suicide, impaired judgment, agitation, psychosis, delirium, delusions, emotional lability, hallucinations, hostility, paranoia, depersonalization, anxiety and depression. Since these are the potential side effects of the drug Eric Harris was taking, it is surprising that in the search for an explanation of the tragedy, more attention has not been drawn to this connection.

During his testimony, Bruce Wiseman, National President of Citizen's Commission on Human Rights (a psychiatric watchdog organization which has been investigating and exposing psychiatric violations of human rights for 30 years), made the following connections between psychiatric drugs and violence in a two year period:

1. On May 25, 1997 18-year-old Jeremy Strohmeyer raped and murdered a 7-year-old African American girl in Las Vegas, Nevada. Strohmeyer had been diagnosed with ADD and prescribed Dexedrine, a Ritalin®-like drug, immediately prior to the killing.

2. On October 1, 1997, in Pearl Mississippi, 16-year-old

Step 1—Understand the Medical System

Luke Woodham stabbed his mother, 50-year-old Mary Woodham, to death and then went to his high school where he shot nine people, killing two teenage girls and wounding seven others. Published reports say he was on Prozac.

3. Exactly two months later on Dec 1, 1997, Michael Carneal, a 14-year-old, opened fire on students at a high school prayer meeting in West Paducah, Kentucky. Three teenagers were killed, five others were wounded, one of whom was paralyzed. Carneal was reportedly on Ritalin®.

4. Then in February 1998, a young man in Huntsville, Alabama on Ritalin® went psychotic chopping up his parents with an ax and also killing one sibling and almost murdering another.

5. On March 24, 1998 in Jonesboro, Arkansas, 11-year-old Andrew Golden and 14-year-old Mitchell Johnson shot 15 people killing four students, one teacher, and wounding 10 others. According to one report, the boys were believed to be on Ritalin®.

6. Two months later another grisly school massacre occurred. On May 21, 1998 15-year-old Kip Kinkel of Springfield, Oregon murdered his parents and proceeded to his high school where he went on a rampage killing two students and wounding 22 others. Kinkel had been prescribed both Prozac and Ritalin®.

7. On April 16, 1999, 15-year-old Shawn Cooper of Notus, Idaho took a 12-gauge shot gun to school and started firing, injuring one student and holding the school hostage for about 20 minutes. Terrified students ran for their lives, some barricading themselves

in classrooms. Cooper had been taking Ritalin® when he fired the shotgun's rounds.

8. Eighteen-year-old Eric Harris killed 12 students and a teacher at Columbine High School before killing himself. Harris was on one of the SSRI anti-depressants called Luvox.

9. A month later to the day, on May 20, 1999 T.J. Solomon, a 15-year-old high school student in Conyers, Georgia, on Ritalin®, opened fire on and wounded six of his classmates. Thankfully, none were killed.

10. Fourteen-year-old Rod Mathews who had been prescribed Ritalin® since the third grade beat a classmate to death with a bat.

11. Nineteen-year-old James Wilson, who had been on psychiatric drugs for 5 years, took a .22 caliber revolver into an elementary school in Breenwood, South Carolina, killing two young girls and wounding seven other children and two teachers.

Based on what the drug companies state about their own drugs, each can cause paranoia or psychotic behaviors. Since so many kids involved in school shootings have been taking psychiatric drugs, I believe every time there is a violent act we should ask if the individuals involved are taking or have been taking psychiatric drugs. So many lives are being destroyed and lost that the question demands an answer. Even if the odds of psychotic or aggressive behaviors from these drugs are very low, the more children who are taking them, the more often we will see an adverse reaction.

Several studies found psychotic symptoms in at least two percent of those taking Ritalin® or amphetamines. With that in mind, consider this:

There are at least five million children taking prescribed Ritalin® or amphetamines today. If two percent have psychotic reactions, that would be 100,000. If only one fourth of one percent (a very small percentage) of these 100,000 psychotic children took a gun to school, that would be 100 acts of violence in our schools. This number seems close to the number of acts of school violence we hear about each week in the news. With these statistics, if I were a teacher, I'd be very concerned, if not outright frightened, to have students in my classroom taking these drugs.

SIDE EFFECTS OF DRUGS USED FOR ADHD

According to the manufacturers' drug inserts and to the PDR, the following are some of the side effects of the drugs commonly used for ADHD.

Amphetamine/amphetamine type

Ritalin®: depression, chronic abuse can lead to tolerance and psychic dependency with varying degrees of abnormal behavior. Frank psychotic episodes can occur. Patients with agitation may react adversely. CBC and platelet count (lab work) are advised. Long-term affects have not been established.
Cardiac side effects: necrotizing vasculitis, thrombocytopenia purpura, blood pressure and pulse changes, rapid heart beat, cardiac arrhythmia, angina.

Adderall: Amphetamine with high potential for abuse, controlled substance, may lead to drug dependence, may exacerbate behavior disturbances and thought disorders,

and psychotic episodes.
Cardiac side effects: palpitations, rapid heartbeat, hypertension, cardiomyopathy with chronic use of amphetamines.

Dexedrine: Amphetamine with high potential for abuse, controlled substance, may lead to drug dependence, psychotic episodes.
Cardiac side effects: palpitations, rapid heartbeat, hypertension, cardiomyopathy with chronic amphetamine use.

Selective Serotonin Reuptake Inhibitors

Prozac: Anxiety, restlessness, mania/hypomania, seizures, suicide, impaired judgment, agitation, amnesia, confusion, emotional lability, apathy, depersonalization, hallucinations, hostility, paranoid reaction, personality disorder, delusions.
Cardiac side effects: hemorrhage, hypertension, angina, arrhythmias, congestive heart failure, heart attack, rapid heart beat, atrial fibrillation, cerebral embolism, heart block.

Zoloft: Mania/hypomania, suicide, agitation, anxiety, emotional lability, apathy, paranoid reactions, hallucinations, aggressive reactions, delusions, illusion.
Cardiac side effects: heart palpitations, chest pain, hypertension, rapid heartbeat, dizziness, syncope, fluid retention, heart attack.

Paxil: Mania/hypomania, impaired judgment, agitation, depression, anxiety, drugged feeling, depersonalization, amnesia, emotional lability, abnormal thinking, hallucinations, lack of emotion, hostility, manic reaction, neurosis, paranoid reaction, antisocial reaction, delirium, delu-

sions, drug dependence, stupor.
Cardiac side effects: hypertension, rapid heartbeat, syncope; EKG abnormalities, angina, heart attack.

Luvox: mania, apathy, amnesia, delusions, depersonalization, drug dependence, emotional lability, hostility, paranoid reaction, and phobia.
Cardiac side effects: hypertension, rapid heartbeat, syncope, angina, heart failure, and heart attack.

OTHER DRUGS

Catapres: Adult high blood pressure drug: delirium, mental depression, visual and auditory hallucinations, restlessness, anxiety, agitation, irritability, other behavioral changes, drowsiness.
Cardiac side-effects: congestive heart failure, cerebrovascular accident (stroke), EKG abnormalities, arrhythmias, chest pain, syncope, high blood pressure, rapid heartbeat and palpitations.

Wellbutrin: Agitation, anxiety, restlessness, delusions, hallucinations, psychotic episodes, confusion, paranoia, mania, seizures, hostility, depression, depersonalization, mood instability, thought disorder, suicidal ideation.
Cardiac side effects: edema, chest pain, EKG abnormalities, shortness of breath, heart attack.

Norpramine: Psychiatric disturbances, seizures, anxiety, hallucinations, restlessness, agitation, nightmares, insomnia, confusion, tremors.
Cardiac side effects: Sudden death in children, heart attack, heart block, stroke, arrhythmias, rapid heart rate.

THE DEBATE GOES TO COURT

At the time of this writing, several lawsuits around the country have been filed and are currently pending involving the makers of Ritalin®. Parents of an 11-year old girl sued Novartis, the manufacturer of Ritalin®, saying the drug company was responsible for their daughter's death after she developed a rapid heartbeat when her doctor increased her dosage. The lawsuit accused the company of producing a defective product and of concealing the adverse reactions and Ritalin®-related deaths.

Three other lawsuits were filed in Texas, California and New Jersey involving several defendants. These lawsuits could be a class-action suit against Novartis and The American Psychiatric Association. The suit in Texas also included the non-profit organization, CHADD. The Texas law suit alleged that these organizations "committed fraud and conspiracy and colluded to create, develop and promote the diagnosis of ADHD and ADD in a highly successful effort to increase the market for its product, Ritalin®." (See the Internet site www.ritalinfraud.com)

DRUG FREE AMERICA?

We would all like to have a drug-free America. We spend a great deal of money and resources to try to prevent and to cure drug abuse and yet the problem persists, even flourishes. I believe the medical establishment's confusing, mixed message presents a major obstacle to this effort. As soon as children are born, the drugging starts. When our babies get their first ear or respiratory infection, the doctors start prescribing antibiotics. As soon as many children reach school age, they are given Ritalin®, Prozac or Adderall. Unfortunately, many are given Ritalin®, Prozac or Adderall, as young as two years of age. As children grow older, teenage girls take appetite suppressants and college students use Ritalin® and other prescribed amphetamines for a quick, cheap high, just as they would use cocaine. Studies have found that Ritalin® is a highly sought-after abused street drug in high school and college. Meanwhile, the harried housewife is on Prozac or another SSRI to treat another psychiatrist-created disorder call Premenstrual Dysphoric Disorder (PMDD). Yes, Sarafem, the "new" drug touted to alleviate the symptoms of PMDD, is just another name for Prozac. The drug company, Eli Lilly, will lose patent protection on Prozac in 2001. However, in July, 2000, the FDA approved Sarafem, which contains the same active ingredient as Prozac, for treatment of Premenstrual Dysphoric Disorder, which provides an opportunity for new patents and new financial protection for an old drug for another fabricated psychiatric diagnosis.

How in the world are we going to have a drug-free America when our medical profession pushes drugs? At best I fear we are teaching our children to turn to drugs to answer their problems; at worst our children are learning this lesson well and becoming addicted.

DRUGS: A QUICK, CHEAP FIX

Another problem of using drugs to cover symptoms is that we stop looking for the real problem and the real solutions. That's what this book is all about, finding and treating the underlying problem instead of covering the symptoms with drugs.

Taking the time to find the underlying causes of a health problem does not fit in the quick, cheap fix, environment of managed care. A drug to cover the symptoms is usually the treatment of choice under the managed care mode. Without doing much else, doctors can prescribe a drug quickly and move on to another patient. Many parents feel pressure to put their child on drugs because most of the time the doctor offers no other options.

UNDERLYING CAUSES OF HEALTH & LEARNING PROBLEMS

Certainly, giving your child amphetamines or speed to promote better behavior not only disregards the possible health problems causing the symptoms, but exposes the child to the many risks of drug therapy. In addition, this approach ultimately discounts these children emotionally and affects their self-esteem because they must wear the ADHD label, a psychiatric diagnosis that can negatively impact them for the rest of their lives.

Every child deserves a complete medical work-up by a physician who understands that allergies, blood sugar problems, learning problems, diet and nutrition can affect how a child feels, thinks and acts.

When a child has attention and behavior problems, it is not ADHD. These kids don't have psychiatric problems. They often have medical conditions or academic problems interfering with their attention and behavior. If a doctor's solution is to write a prescription, I recommend to my patients that they find a doctor who knows how to look for the underlying cause of the problem. If a doctor prescribes a drug, I always ask the pharmacist for the drug insert to learn what the possible side effects can be. I adhere to the "worst case scenario" philosophy. If a certain side effect can occur, it might just happen to me or to my child. I ask myself if the problem I am dealing with is worth having one or more of the listed side effects. Would I rather deal more effectively with the problem and try to fix it or risk the occurrence of the side effects? It is my right as a patient or parent of a patient to make this decision. Be sure to take the time to thoroughly educate yourself so you are comfortable with your decision.

Step 1—Understand the Medical System

Remember:

- A doctor can be strongly influenced by the pharmaceutical industry.
- If a doctor's only tool is a prescription pad then all anyone will ever get is a drug.
- The importance of a complete history and physical exam.
- The importance of considering all possible underlying causes.
- The importance of knowing all possible side effects of a recommended treatment.
- ADHD is a psychiatric label.
- Ritalin® and cocaine are very similar.
- There is no valid test to diagnose ADHD.
- There is no data proving ADHD is a brain dysfunction.
- All the drugs that are currently used for attention and behavior can cause heart problems and psychotic or paranoid behaviors.

STEP 2—EDUCATE YOURSELF ON THE SCHOOL SYSTEM

WHERE ARE YOU?

You are taken into a room and made to sit in a hard wooden chair with a bar in front of it. You are not allowed to eat, to drink, to speak, or to go to the bathroom. And if you cannot follow these rules you are given psychiatric drugs to control your behavior. Where are you? In a prison? No, you are in an American public elementary school! When you strip away your mental vision of what school is supposed to be, you can begin to see the stark reality.

Certainly there must be rules and guidelines as well as conformity in order to teach so many students everyday. Although there are many wonderful teachers and schools where learning is enjoyable, the basic classroom structure is not comfortable. I couldn't sit in an office all day under those conditions and be productive, much less be able to learn. Yet we expect children as young as six and seven to do just that. Children are supposed to be active; not just a little active, but very active. That's how they learn and grow. Yet, we put them in situations that are contrary to their basic nature. Then when they are unable to control their physiological need to be active, we drug them.

THE PROBLEM WITH SCHOOLS

I truly believe that teachers today are underpaid and over-worked and a great deal is expected of them. That being said, I also believe that it is the public educational system that has helped to bring on this epidemic of drugging our children. Schools want children to meet their standards no matter how unrealistic and inappropriate those standards may be. In addition, the schools are making it even harder on the children to get a break from the classroom structure.

I know in Texas many schools have eliminated the Physical Education (PE) programs and they are eliminating or dramatically cutting recess time. Many others are even requiring silent lunch periods, where children are either not allowed to speak or may only speak for brief time periods. One parent told me that the bus ride to and from school is expected to be silent. When are our children supposed to learn socialization? When are they supposed to let loose? The kids who need to "run off" energy the most are often kept inside during recess as punishment for their overactive classroom behavior. Does the teacher actually think that they are going to be able to act better in the afternoon after so many restrictions?

We need to recognize that children are children, not little adults. They are active and inquisitive and need a lot of physical activity for their own development. It is a basic necessity. I know I couldn't sit in a chair all day at my age. Certainly children, with their immature nervous systems, should not be expected to sit quietly at their desks for most of the day.

One child I saw at my office had problems concentrating

because his teacher required him to keep both feet on the floor at all times during class. The mother explained to the teacher that her child always studied at home with his legs curled up under him because he could concentrate better in that position. The teacher would not yield on this point and at the same time complained that the child had attention and learning problems in class. The teacher recommended that the child be tested for ADHD. Instead the mother brought her child to me. I wrote a prescription that he be allowed to put his legs under him during class. The child's grades and learning improved. It was such a simple thing to do and the results were excellent. I find in my practice that many of the problems these children experience in school can be remedied if the teacher and the school system consider differences in learning styles.

THE ADHD LABEL MEANS MONEY, MONEY, MONEY

The consumption of Ritalin® spiked from 1992 to 1996 along with the application of the ADHD label. The huge increase in Ritalin® prescriptions coincides with ADHD qualifying as a disability and falling under the protection of the Americans with Disabilities Act (ADA). Every time a child becomes labeled as ADHD, the schools qualify to receive extra funding. In theory, this is to provide special services to meet the ADHD disabled child's needs.

Even if a school receives additional moneys for an ADHD child, the school can simply dispense a drug to the child. To actually help the child with the learning problems would cost the school more money. This government funding for the ADHD label provides a stronger incentive to diagnose a child with ADHD than to apply the usual classroom resources to help a child learn.

Parents often feel a tremendous amount of pressure from the teachers to drug their children. The families who come to my office often report similar stories. Soon after starting school, the teacher notifies the parents their child fidgets and has difficulty sitting still and paying attention. Soon after these reports begin, the teacher tells the parents they should see a doctor to have their child evaluated. Even though it is illegal for teachers to tell parents to medicate their child, some teachers are either unaware of this law or totally disregard it.

Many teachers will come right out and tell parents the child should be medicated. Others will be a little more subtle. A teacher might say, "I've seen so many children improve on Ritalin®. They acted just like your child until they started on Ritalin®. Now they're doing great." Another might give the parent the name of a doctor with a reputation for handing out Ritalin® prescriptions. I have spoken with parents who followed up on the teacher's recommendation. When their child's pediatrician said the child did not have ADHD and should not be drugged, the teacher actually told the parents to get a second opinion and gave them the name of a physician who had readily prescribed a psychiatric drug to other children in the class.

COURT-ORDERED RITALIN®!

In a case in the state of New York that made national news, parents were forced to put their child on Ritalin® against their wishes. The issue was brought to the courts after a teacher turned in the parents to Child Protective Services for medical negligence when they stopped the child's Ritalin®. I never thought that in America we would see parents' rights replaced with court-ordered Ritalin®!

Not a day goes by, it seems, that I do not hear a similar story. It seems as if our schools have turned into psychiatric hospitals instead of places of learning. Parents send their children off each morning to be educated, not to be drugged. Many teachers may be reading this and thinking that I am completely wrong. Of course these things do not occur in every classroom or in every school. But it does happen in far too many school situations. I believe that many teachers and other school personnel have forgotten what it means to be a child. Personally, I am more concerned about the child who can sit still in this environment than one who cannot.

RITALIN® DOES NOT ENHANCE LEARNING

Though a drug like Ritalin® may cause the child to sit still longer and to focus more (just as an amphetamine would) it does not mean the drug is correcting a problem or helping to improve academic performance. It may surprise many to know that studies have found that children who take amphetamine-type or other mind-altering drugs do not perform better academically. Yes, according to the NIH report, no studies indicate enhanced academic performance from these drugs. Studies found that children who take these drugs fail just as many courses and drop out of school just as often as children who did not take the drugs.

Someone is benefiting from this drugging of children but it's not the children. The pharmaceutical companies, doctors, and schools benefit – all financially. Teachers can benefit in another way. It is certainly going to be a lot easier to handle a group of kids drugged into compliance. It would make the teacher's day easier if mind-altering drugs controlled the behavior of any of the children who might be a little too active. No rocket science degree needed to see the advantage here.

BELIEVING IN THE ADHD MYTH

Many parents are quite happy to drug their children. Believing the ADHD diagnosis has some basis in fact, they are often thrilled to find out there is not only a reason for their child's behavior, but also a treatment. If early on they see dramatic improvement in the child's behavior they become convinced that ADHD is real and the drug is actually the cure. Unfortunately, these parents may be losing important time in actually going after the real cause of the problem. It is much easier to work with young children in finding the underlying cause and fixing it than it is to work with teenagers. By the time parents discover that the drug did not do everything they expected, their child is a teenager with many years of problems behind them.

SCHOOLS EXERT PRESSURE

When school personnel pressure parents to drug their child it can be very difficult to go against them. They have your child all day and the teacher's attitude toward the child will influence the child's self-esteem and educational future. Too many times I have been told of situations in which the teacher was determined to have the child drugged. The teacher looked negatively at every little thing the child did. Even when other children in the classroom were behaving the same way, the child who the teacher wanted drugged would be the only one to get singled out and in trouble. The child's behaviors were constantly reported to the parents. In some situations, the other children in the classroom would tell their own parents that this other child was being picked on by the teacher. To me the teacher is holding the child hostage and has the ability to harm the child if the parents do not agree to do what the teacher wants.

Young children have great difficulty understanding all of this. They cannot possibly know why they get in trouble for the same behaviors others can do without retribution. Self-esteem suffers. I remember a five-year-old boy in his first semester of kindergarten who already hated school. When this little guy walked into my office I was really taken by him. He was quite adorable and talkative. He was very bright and had lots of questions. I thought it a shame this precious boy, in just a few short months, had come to dislike school so much. It turns out the child's teacher expected him to sit quietly most of the day. Whenever he could not do what was so inappropriately expected of him, the teacher scolded him or sent him to the principal's office. It did not take this little boy long to realize that the teacher did not accept him for who he was. The teacher continued this behavior until the parents gave in and put the child on Ritalin®. Only then did the teacher stop harassing him. His mother reported to me that she could see no difference in her child's behavior on the Ritalin®. All the drug had done was get the teacher to stop attacking her son. She brought him to my office to see if there was a safer approach than using the mind-altering drug.

WHEN PRESSURE DOESN'T WORK, CALL IN CPS

Some schools have become very aggressive about forcing parents to drug their children. They focus on the child's every move, reporting each detail to the parents. Both the child and the parents become so intimidated they often will do what the teacher wants just to make it stop. Some parents are stronger, though. They do not give in to the teacher's demands. In some cases, school personnel contacted Child Protective Services (CPS) alleging medical negligence when parents refused to drug a child.

THE STORY OF TWO FAMILIES

There were two such incidences reported in the August 8, 2000 issue of *USA Today* that occurred in the state of New York. In one case, the parents were taken to court where it was ruled that the parents must drug their child. The second case was a patient of mine. I tell their story with permission from the mother.

Michael had actually been on several different psychiatric drugs in the past. He had adverse reactions to all of them. His behavior on the drugs was potentially dangerous and alarmed his parents. They tried several different drugs but each caused even worse problems. Finally, they decided to stop the drugs all together. When they did so, the school personnel turned them in to CPS. They had already decided to travel to my office in the Dallas/Fort Worth area from New York to see if I could help them. They told the school they were going to Texas, but the school did not wait. Even though the school called CPS before the family could leave town, they were still able to leave New York and come to Texas for Michael's evaluation and treatment plan. What I found was very interesting.

LOOKING FOR THE UNDERLYING CAUSES

Michael's mom sent all of his medical records to me to review. I was stunned. Here was a child who had been prescribed many psychiatric drugs, sometimes two at a time, yet not one single doctor had ever taken the time to do a physical exam. No doctor had drawn blood to see if he had any medical condition that could be evaluated through the blood. The doctors just kept prescribing drug after drug, even though Michael continued to have adverse reactions to them.

In my office, I found Michael had several medical conditions that could have caused his symptoms. To begin with, he was anemic. Iron deficiency or anemia has been associated with symptoms that could be mislabeled as ADHD. He was also low in specific nutrients, especially magnesium. Magnesium deficiency is associated with excessive fidgeting, anxious restlessness, psychomotor instability and learning difficulties. Finally, Michael had many allergies, which have been associated with cognitive dysfunction. He had learning differences as well. (Each of these issues will be discussed in greater detail later in this book.)

FINDING THE UNDERLYING CAUSES

Michael's medical and educational problems interfered with his ability to function optimally at school. Yet no other doctor even bothered to look for these things. Instead he was continually prescribed psychiatric drugs that caused serious side effects. When I reported these findings to his school, they did not care. They refused to ac-

cept my evaluation and instead told Michael's parents
that they must take Michael to a psychiatrist. His parents
found a psychiatrist that was not "drug happy" to evaluate
Michael. With this psychiatrist's report in hand, CPS
backed off. Michael's parents removed him from the
school and placed him in a combination of private school
and home schooling where he is doing just fine.

A RIGHT TO DRUG-FREE EDUCATION

Parents should not be put through this sort of ordeal.
They should certainly have the right to decide if they want
their child drugged or not. Think about what we know to
be true:

1. There is no objective way to diagnose ADHD.
2. The drugs used to "treat" ADHD can cause heart prob-
    lems and adverse behavior.
3. The drugs do not help all of the symptoms.
4. There are no long-term studies on the safety or effi-
    cacy of the drugs.
5. Many of the drugs used have never been tested on
    children.

With this information, it seems outrageous to me that the
schools are allowed so much control over parent's rights.
In the United States, every child has a right to a public
education. To me this does not mean that every child has
a right to a public education only if the child is taking psychiatric drugs. Many of our schools are more like psychiatric institutions than institutions of education.

THE SCHOOL VS. PARENT RIGHTS

When I was giving a talk in Dallas, a woman told me her child's school turned her into Child Protective Services for not putting her child on Ritalin®. She was forced to defend herself in court where she was told she would lose her child if she did not accept the Ritalin® treatment. Her child had suffered previous adverse side effects to the drug. That fact apparently did not concern either the school, Child Protective Services or the court. This incident was very similar to the case in New York. I see families from all over the United States, and this collaboration between the schools and Child Protective Services to force parents to drug their children is widespread.

STATE SCHOOL BOARDS TAKING ACTION

After the killings at Columbine High School in Colorado, the Colorado State School Board conducted hearings to look at the possible negative effects of placing children on psychiatric drugs for school. During the hearings, experts reported that many of these psychiatric drugs could cause violent and suicidal behaviors as adverse side effects. As mentioned, Eric Harris had been taking Luvox, which can cause these adverse behaviors and many other nervous system reactions, according to the drug's manufacturer. The Colorado School Board was particularly interested in the increased number of children taking Ritalin®.

At the same time, a Colorado legislative committee was meeting on the same topic. I testified at the legislative hearings about the problems with Ritalin® and other psychiatric drugs and explained that there are effective alternatives to drugs. The results of the school board hearing were encouraging. The board passed a resolution stating that teachers and school administrators should look for educational means to handle problems in school and not push parents to put their children on drugs. Other states, including Texas, have followed suit. [See Figure 4, Colorado State Board of Education Resolution.]

It is possible to promote change within the school system for the benefit of our children. At the hearings in Texas, Gretchen Feussner, a pharmacist with the DEA, stated some surveys show that up to 20% of children admitted to recreational abuse of their prescription stimulant drugs.

NO WIGGLING ALLOWED

I live in Fort Worth, Texas and my office is in the Dallas/Fort Worth area. In 1999 the Fort Worth Independent School District brought in outside consultants to look at their Special Education Programs. Remember, ADHD falls under Special Education. After inspecting the school classrooms, the consultants found that phonics is better than whole language, yet whole language is still being used. They discovered more time and energy being spent trying to label children as special education students than in trying to help them. Many children were being labeled as Special Education simply to get them out of the classroom with no consideration of the child's history or of the parents' opinion. So even if something serious might be occurring at home with a child, those circumstances were not taken into consideration. The consultants also found that most of the psychological testing was not necessary or even required. (I tell parents that they don't have to let the school psychologically test their child. It has been my experience that when the schools test these children or refer these children for testing, the children almost always end up with the ADHD diagnosis and a prescription for

---

Figure 4

Colorado State Board of Education
RESOLUTION
Promoting The Use Of Academic Solutions To Resolve
Problems With Behavior, Attention, And Learning

Whereas, the Colorado State Board of Education is constitutionally charged with the general supervision of K-12 public education; and,

Whereas, the Colorado State Board of Education dedicates itself to increasing academic achievement levels for all students; and,

Whereas, the responsibility of school personnel is to ensure student achievement; and,

Whereas, only medical personnel can recommend the use of prescription medications; and,

Whereas, the Colorado State Board of Education recognizes that there is much concern regarding the issue of appropriate and thorough diagnosis and medication and their impact on student achievement; and,

Whereas, there are documented incidences of highly negative consequences in which psychiatric prescription drugs have been utilized for what are essentially problems of discipline which may be related to lack of academic success;

Therefore Be It Resolved, that the Colorado State Board of Education encourage school personnel to use proven academic and/or classroom management solutions to resolve behavior, attention, and learning difficulties; and,

Be It Further Resolved, that the Colorado State Board of Education encourage greater communication and education among parents, educators, and medical professionals about the effects of psychotropic drugs on student achievement and our ability to provide a safe and civil learning environment.

November 11, 1999

Ritalin® or Adderall or another psychiatric drug.)

Additionally, the consultants found a disproportionate number of African American students in the learning disability category. Seventy percent of those labeled learning disabled should not have been and were not receiving the help they needed. They reported that 40% of the students were referred to Special Education for behavior alone and little effort was made to find ways to deal with them. Half the schools in the district referred 10-26% of their students for special education. And finally, the consultants

---

Figure 5

Fort Worth Independent School District
Consultant Report Overview

- Schools spend more time and energy labeling children than helping them
- Teachers refer children to Special Education to get them out of their classroom
- Most tests administered are not necessary or legally required
- 70% should not have been labeled learning disabled and did not get the help they needed
- 40% referred for behavior problems and little effort made to deal them
- 10-26% of student population in special education
- A disproportionate number of African-American students are labeled learning disabled
- Special education is given a low priority
- Parents views are not always considered
- Low tolerance for wiggling

Fort Worth Star Telegram, July 29, 1999

---

reported a low tolerance for wiggling. Based on the stories I hear from families all over this county and the world, I don't think the Fort Worth Independent School District is all that different from any other school system.

RITALIN® OR PLACEBO?

Parents often tell me their child has a wonderful year with one teacher only to have a difficult year the next with a different teacher. During the difficult year, the teacher will pressure the parents to put their child on drugs. I find that quite often the problem is not with the child but with the teacher's expectation of the child. If the teacher expects the child to be a problem, the teacher sees a problem. I have worked with several parents, who, in the face of pressure from a teacher to drug a child, used a placebo instead. The parent gave their child a vitamin in the morning and informed the teacher the child had taken his medication. Would you believe that four out of five teachers said the student was doing significantly better on the placebo? The only difference was that the teacher <u>thought</u> the child was taking a psychiatric drug.

PARENTS—KNOW YOUR RIGHTS

It is against the law for teachers or other school administrators to recommend drugging children. Parents should read carefully all of the paperwork the school asks them to sign. One parent signed paperwork thinking he was giving permission for the school to test his child for speech problems. The papers mentioned other tests but the school said they wanted only to test for speech, so the parent signed the release form. The school tested the child and reported the child did not need speech therapy, but had several other problems for which a pediatrician should prescribe psychiatric drugs.

TESTING THE STUDENT
FOR TEACHER ACCOUNTABILITY

Texas has put in place mandatory academic testing of school children referred to as "accountability." The state rates school administrators and teachers based on student test performance. If the students do well, the teacher can receive a raise and the school more funding. Unfortunately the priority can then become the test results, not how well the children are actually learning.

I have had many teachers and parents tell me schools focus so much on this test some children may be classified as developmentally delayed or diagnosed with learning problems to prevent that child from taking the test and lowering the school's scores. According to reports by parents and teachers, some children are told to stay home on test day for the same reason.

The CBS News program *60 Minutes* reported in September, 2000 that teachers and administrators were caught cheating to ensure that their school received a good score. Many teachers have written to the local newspaper to report inequities of this "accountability" testing. This "accountability" is now a goal of a national education plan. I have serious concerns that this will result in an even greater increase in the drugging of school children.

PRIVATE SCHOOLS

Private schools are not always better. Several parents reported to me that a religious school in the area had hired a psychiatrist to prescribe drugs to whichever children the teachers wanted drugged. If the parents did not agree, they could take their children elsewhere. Not all private schools have this attitude, but finding out the percentage of children at a given school taking psychiatric drugs is a good indicator of the school's philosophy.

HOME SCHOOLING

I often recommend Home Schooling for children. I used to think home schooled children did not get enough socialization. I know now that this is not the case. Most children at home can complete their assignments in three to four hours, then have the rest of the day to do activities with other home-schooled children. These children appear to have more self-confidence and better self-esteem. When a child is being tormented by a school situation in which the teacher wants the child drugged, they often will do much better when removed from that antagonizing situation.

WHO HAS ADHD: THE STUDENT OR THE TEACHER?

Recently a mother and son came to my office. This was their story: "My seven-year-old son has never had any problems in school. Last year he had a wonderful year with a wonderful teacher. This year he has two teachers. One is also wonderful and he is having a great year with him with no problems at all. He makes good grades in his class and enjoys learning there. But his other teacher is quite different. In her class, my son is always in trouble. The teacher admits that she has trouble sitting still and is glad that she is the teacher and can move around. She says she could never sit still in the little chairs all day. Her classroom is hectic and unorganized. The children do not know what is expected of them. My son does not do well in this classroom with this teacher and his grades reflect that.

"This second teacher is continually sending notes home to me reporting that my son is misbehaving in class. To be fair, I took my son to a counselor to see if there was something wrong with him. The counselor requested that the two teachers fill out the Connor's Rating Scale on my son. The differences in the results were dramatic. The first teacher rated my son very low. However, the second teacher, the one who had already reported to me that my son misbehaves in class, not surprisingly, rated my son very high. This was the counselor's assessment: 'If your son had two teachers like the first one who rated him very low, he would not have ADHD. If he had two teachers like the second, who rated him very high, he would have ADHD. But since he has one of each, he is just Borderline ADHD'."

Now this is a perfect example of the subjective and invalid nature of the ADHD diagnosis. It would not mean that this boy was ADHD if two teachers gave him a high evaluation. It would simply mean he had two inferior teachers. Let's not blame the child for the shortcomings of the teacher. All of our children should have "two good teachers" so then there could be No More ADHD.

Step 2—Educate Yourself on the School System

Remember:

- The schools can receive government funds for each child labeled ADHD.
- It is illegal for teachers and other school personnel to tell parents that they should medicate their children.
- Many states have passed a resolution recommending that schools promote academic solutions instead of drugs.
- The importance of knowing federal and state laws and rights.
- It is not required to let the school psychologically test a child.

STEP 3— DUMP THE SUGAR

Yes, sugar does affect behavior. Sugar affects children even more then it does adults. Ask teachers, they know. Parents know too. Many studies support this fact. It makes perfectly good sense to me because it's basic physiology. Yet many doctors, who went to medical school where physiology is a required course, dispute this fact.

BASIC PHYSIOLOGY

If we look at basic physiology, it is hard to prove that sugar does not affect behavior. Eating sugar or foods containing a lot of sugar results in high sugar levels in the blood. The body then releases insulin to take the sugar or glucose to our cells. If too much glucose is taken from the blood, the blood sugar level drops, resulting in hypoglycemia or low blood sugar, which can cause attention and behavior symptoms often labeled ADHD. When the body becomes hypoglycemic, the chemical adrenaline is released which, when dumped into a child's blood stream, causes the "fight or flight" energy surge.

THE ADRENALINE SURGE

The body releases the hormone adrenaline as a protective measure. If you are walking down the street and someone jumps out at you with a gun or a knife, adrenaline comes to your rescue. It goes to your arms and legs and allows you to run faster or fight harder in response to the dangerous situation. We have all heard stories about a mother who managed to lift a car when her child was lying under it. Adrenaline gave the mother the extra inhuman strength to do the impossible. We would not want to eliminate adrenaline and its ability to protect us from danger, but we do want to control it so that it is not released at inappropriate times to interfere with our everyday lives or with the ability of our children to concentrate and behave.

DR. JEKYLL AND MR. HYDE BEHAVIORS

The term "Jekyll and Hyde" has often been used in association with children with behavior problems. One minute they are sweet, nice and calm, and then the next they turn into monsters. Most of the time I find adrenaline to be the culprit. When adrenaline is released "Mr. Hyde" is on the loose. When the adrenaline leaves the child's blood stream, nice "Dr. Jekyll" returns.

Even if the child is sitting comfortably in the classroom, trying to pay attention, an adrenaline release can have a profound effect. The pupils in the eyes dilate; the heart rate increases and the child cannot sit still. Studies have shown that if your heart is beating fast, you cannot concentrate or focus. The child can become agitated. Any little thing can now trigger the child to act angrily or even aggressively. Such behavior is not conscious. The child does not choose to act that way. It is a physiological reaction. The adrenaline release occurs out of a natural protective mechanism activated, not by danger or fear, but by what the child eats. The adrenaline causes the agitation, irritability and shakiness that the child may feel.

CAUSES OF LOW BLOOD SUGAR

Low blood sugar can occur in two different ways. When we eat sugar and it enters the blood stream, insulin also enters and grabs the sugar to take it to the cells to be used. This can leave too little sugar in the bloodstream resulting in low blood sugar or hypoglycemia. Adrenaline is then released, resulting in the symptoms most often referred to as ADHD such as agitation, aggression, irritability, shakiness, inability to sit still and craving of more sugar.

The second way to have a low blood sugar is to not eat often enough and when you do eat, to not eat enough protein. Proteins are meats, eggs, cheese, and nuts. To protect a child from having a low blood sugar response, I have them remove all sugar, all sweets and all white grains such as white bread, pasta and rice. These white grains are turned into sugar very quickly after they are eaten, so the body thinks more sugar was just ingested. A diet higher in protein and lower in carbohydrates can help keep the blood sugar stabilized. [*See Figure 6*, Low Refined Carbohydrate Eating Plan.]

In addition to eliminating the sugar, I recommend the child eat every 2 to 2 1/2 hours. They must include some form of protein with each meal or snack. Doing these two things can significantly help stabilize blood sugar levels and keep a child off the roller coaster of low blood sugar/adrenaline behaviors. [*See Figure 7.*]

SUGAR STUDIES

I have heard many doctors quote studies that say that sugar does not affect behavior. I have a problem with the

Figure 6

Low Refined Carbohydrate Eating Plan

Breakfast
Eggs, bacon, sausage, soy, chicken, turkey, beef, pork, fish (sausage and bacon should be nitrate/nitrite-free)
Water to drink (glass-bottled spring or filtered water)

Mid-morning snack
Nut butter, if not allergic (peanut, almond, cashew butter) on whole grain or sprouted wheat bread or crackers, meat or fish sandwich (meat loaf, tuna, chicken salad), cheese, trail mix without candy (dried fruit is okay.)
Water to drink

Lunch
School lunches, milk if not allergic (white milk only, no chocolate. Water would be a better choice)
Real juice (no added sugar) to drink
Plain corn or potato chips (without added chemicals, preservatives or colors)
Vegetables would be a good addition
Whole fruit instead of sweet dessert
Find out what your child is really eating at lunch-if it is just chips or French fries and dessert, this is a problem.

Afternoon Snack
Same as morning snack

Dinner
Meat (chicken, turkey, beef, pork)
Vegetables, cooked or raw, salads
Potato, brown rice, whole grain pasta (Limit potato to three times per week.)

Figure 6—Cont'd

Water or real juice to drink
Fruit instead of sweet dessert

Evening Snack
Same as other snacks. (Can add popcorn or unsweetened cereal but must have some form of protein also.)
Water to drink

Encourage protein intake (eggs, meat, fish, soy)
Discourage sugar, sweets intake
Occasional sweets OK if eaten after a full meal with protein (occasional means for special occasions like birthdays)
Drink 8-8 ounce glasses water daily (2 liters). Filtered or glass bottled spring water
Breads, cereals, crackers, pasta, rolls should be whole grain or sprouted, not white or caramel-colored white flour
Use organic foods whenever possible

Figure 7

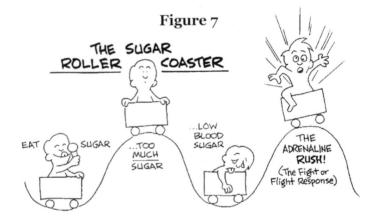

studies I have seen which express this point of view. It has been reported that no difference occurred in children who did or did not have sugar; however, it appears that the researchers used fructose and sucrose interchangeably. Now that you have read about the effects of adrenaline, I believe you will understand why I do not think those particular studies are valid. Fructose and sucrose are metabolized very differently in the body. Sucrose can cause the insulin/adrenaline roller coaster while fructose does not. If these two types of sugars were used interchangeably in the studies, it is easy to see why the studies are flawed and the results inaccurate.

Also, in studies where aspartame was used as a sugar substitute, there was no discussion concerning the possible neurological effect of aspartame. In my practice I have seen aspartame cause migraine headaches and seizures. In my opinion, anything that can cause such a powerful effect on the nervous system would not be a fair or valid substitute in this type of research. Another bit of information not usually made public concerns the sponsors of the studies. If the sugar industry financed the study, the results might very well end up being favorable to sugar.

THE YALE STUDY

A study that did show a correlation between sugar and behavior was conducted at Yale University. Researchers fed equivalent amounts of sugar to adults and to children on a percentage of body weight. Blood glucose levels and blood adrenaline levels were measured every half hour for five hours. The adrenaline levels in the children were ten times higher than normal up to five hours after ingesting the sugar. All of the children in the study had symptoms of increased adrenaline, while only one of the adults did.

Figure 8

Sugar Studies

- Sucrose: may cause a ten times increase in adrenaline levels in children resulting in difficulty concentrating, irritability and anxiety. (Jones, Tini, W. Borg, et al. *Journal of Pediatrics*, I part 2 no. 126 (February 1995): 171-177.)
- Sucrose: may cause increase in inappropriate behavior and decrement in performance. (*Journal of Abnormal Child Psychology,*14 no. 4 (1986): 565-577.)
- Sucrose: Overly aggressive behavior may be associated with elevated sugar intake. (Schauss, A. G. *Diet, Crime and Delinquency*, Berkeley: Parker House, 1980.)

It appears that sugar has a stronger affect on children than on adults. The children in the study were not children labeled with ADHD. I suspect that children with behavior problems might show even greater effects. Another study published in *The Journal of Abnormal Child Psychology* found that sucrose (sugar) may cause an increase in inappropriate behavior and may cause a decrease in performance. Another reported increased sugar intake might cause aggressive behaviors. [*See Figure 8* on Sugar Studies.]

I have seen more than one pre-diabetic or diabetic child in my practice. Parents of these children had been told the child had ADHD and should be on Ritalin®. These children did not have ADHD and Ritalin® would have been a very inappropriate treatment for them. Because they were diabetic, their blood sugar levels were high one minute and low the next. These changes caused the child's attention and behavior problems. One child's behavior was so severe that the child's doctor had recommended he be placed in a psychiatric hospital. All he needed was to have his blood sugar under control with a proper diet and insulin program.

HYPOGLYCEMIA QUICK REVIEW

The treatment for hypoglycemia is simple. Change the child's diet. Make sure the child never gets hungry and eliminate refined carbohydrates, such as candy, cakes, pies and soft drinks from the child's diet. I have seen dramatic results in my patients who have removed sugar from their diets. Parents and teachers have reported improved behavior and concentration. It's an easy thing to do and it doesn't cost a cent. I have included several of my favorite non-sugar recipes that can help to replace the sugary foods that are removed from the diet.

NON-SUGAR TREATS RECIPES
DEVELOPED BY DR. MARY ANN BLOCK

Chocolate-Covered Almonds
2 squares unsweetened chocolate, 2 Tbs. butter, ½ tsp. water
Melt above together in microwave (about one minute).
Add 15 drops liquid stevia and one tsp. vanilla extract .
Mix all together.
Add 16 ounces unsalted, roasted almonds. Mix until almonds are completely coated.
Spread on sheet of wax paper. Refrigerate. When hard, place in bag or other container but keep refrigerated.

Cheese Cake

Crust:

8 ounces crushed nuts of your choice (almonds, pecans, walnuts)(can mix types of nuts and even add a little unsweetened coconut if you like)

25 drops liquid stevia

2 tsps. vanilla

2 Tbls. melted butter

1 egg, mixed

Mix all the above until well blended.

Butter a 9-inch round pie pan. Press nut mixture into bottom and sides of pie plate. Bake at 350° for 10 minutes.

Cream Cheese Mix:

24 ounces cream cheese softened, ¾ pound soft tofu, 30 drops liquid stevia, 1 Tbls. vanilla

Mix in processor until well blended and smooth. Add 2 eggs and blend until smooth. Pour into crust. Bake at 350° for 40 minutes. Refrigerate 3 hours or overnight.

Topping:

Blend 10 strawberries in processor until smooth. Top cheesecake with a layer of strawberries.

Chocolate Peanut Butter Coconut Balls

Melt together 1 square unsweetened chocolate, 1 Tbs. butter and ½ tsp. Water.

Add 10 drops liquid stevia, 1 tsp vanilla extract, 6 Tbs. peanut butter, 3 Tbs. coconut. Mix well. Roll in 1-inch balls. Finely process 3 Tbs. coconut. Roll balls in fine coconut until coated. Refrigerate.

Chocolate Mousse

2 squares unsweetened chocolate melted in double boiler with:

2 Tbs. butter and 1 tsp. water
When melted, mix thoroughly and add:
1 Tbs. vanilla extract
15 drops liquid stevia
Mix well and remove from heat.
Add 8 ounces cream cheese, mix thoroughly.
Whip small container whipping cream until stiff. Fold chocolate mixture into whip cream until well blended. Place in individual containers and refrigerate or freeze. Serve cold. If frozen, allow to thaw slightly before serving.

Icing
8 ounces cream cheese, softened
2 tsp. vanilla extract
20 drops liquid stevia
Combine above and blend well.
Add small amount of milk if too thick.
Can add more stevia or vanilla to taste but do so slowly and cautiously as they can easily be over done.
Can add food coloring also

SUGAR SUBSTITUTES

There are several tasty sugar substitutes available today. They are:

1. Fructose: Fructose does not cause the insulin/ adrenalin reaction. Since most fructose is corn-based, a child who is allergic to corn may continue to react to foods when the fructose is present.
2. Stevia: Stevia is a natural substance that is very sweet. It does not affect blood sugar but it takes some practice to learn to work with it.
3. Xylitol: Xylitol is another natural sweetener. Too

much Xylitol can cause gas or diarrhea but it works well in small amounts.

OTHER SWEET ALTERNATIVES

Frozen fruit and frozen concentrated fruit juices make excellent sweeteners, especially concentrated apple juice and pineapple juice.

Freezing fruit makes a great substitute for ice cream or sherbet.

A frozen banana pushed through a juicer or mashed in a blender or processor tastes just like banana ice cream to me. Frozen grapes and pineapple chunks are delicious, too.

Once sugar is out of the diet completely, it becomes easier to keep it out. Fruits begin to taste much sweeter and more satisfying.

Leaving a small amount of sugar in the diet actually makes it more difficult to follow the diet plan. Sugar can be very addictive. Like any addictive substance, it is easier to avoid if it is avoided 100%. Using even small amounts can tend to keep the craving active, in which case there is a tendency to gradually increase the amount of sugar until it is back to the amount of original consumption.

Step 3—Dump the Sugar

Remember:

- Sugar <u>does</u> effect behavior.
- It is important to remove all sodas, candy, cakes, and pies from the diet.
- It is important to eat three meals and three snacks a day, each of which includes protein.
- The importance of avoiding aspartame as a sugar substitute.

STEP 4— TAKE YOUR ABCs, VITAMINS, THAT IS

A DEMAND FOR A HEALTHY DIET

Consider that perhaps **ADHD** doesn't actually stand for **A**ttention **D**eficit **H**yperactivity **D**isorder but really means **A D**emand for a **H**ealthy **D**iet. Many children's diets are shameful. Sweetened cereals are still the most popular breakfast item. A young father told me he was giving a talk at his children's school and asked their favorite and least favorite foods. Of course the obvious favorites were cookies and candy and the least favorites broccoli and spinach. He then asked what they ate for breakfast and they mentioned several sweetened cereals.

Just because these products are on our grocer's shelves does not mean they provide appropriate nutrition for our children. When you learn more about nutrition and read the labels of the foods you serve to your children, you may have a very different opinion of these products. Sometimes it is very obvious that a child's diet is the problem. For instance, when I was taking a diet history from a mother who brought her child in to see me for severe behavior problems, I asked what the child ate for breakfast. Her response was, "A Tylenol® and a Coke®." Well, that one was easy to fix! But still, trying to feed your child a healthy diet may not be so easy. I am not sure Americans even recognize a healthy diet.

WHAT IS GOOD NUTRITION?

Who gets to decide what good nutrition is? Some would say we have the Five Basic Food Groups as a guide. This is the pyramid that tells us how we should be eating. As with the influence of the pharmaceutical industry, I remain skeptical that the food pyramid was made without the influence of those companies who have much to gain by their products being included in the list. The dairy industry has done an excellent job of marketing their product to the public. It is not unusual for me to hear from parents who are concerned that their child does not like milk. Many parents believe cow's milk is a food we must have.

Actually, humans do not need to drink the milk from another animal. There are many other foods that are good sources of calcium. Milk is not the only or even the best source. As a general population there is a feeling that our bones will crumble if we don't drink three glasses of cow's milk each day. This is just not true. We can obtain calcium from many different sources including salmon, broccoli, calcium fortified fruit juices, soy and rice milk, and supplementation. As I have already discussed in Step 1, someone else may be placing their own financial interests ahead of those of our health. Our knowledge of biochemistry and nutrition is a far better and more accurate guide for health than a familiar marketing campaign.

DIABETES AND THE MILK CONNECTION

If anyone needs another reason to avoid cow's milk products, consider the relationship between Type I, Juvenile Onset, Diabetes and the ingestion of cow's milk. The consumption of cow's milk may actually increase the risk of developing Type I Diabetes. Antibodies from the milk appear to cause an auto-immune reaction against the pancreas in susceptible individuals. The problem is no one knows if they are susceptible until someone else in the family gets diabetes.

FDA GUIDELINES

The FDA's guidelines do not necessarily list recommendations that may be adequate for optimal health. The FDA's minimum nutritional requirements are based on the amount of nutrients needed to prevent diseases such as rickets, scurvy and pellagra. They do not take into account the modern day problems and symptoms that may be caused by nutritional deficiencies. In conventional medicine, these deficiencies are treated with drugs to cover up the symptoms. Most physicians are not looking for nutritional deficiencies as the underlying cause of health problems.

Looking for the underlying cause of a problem will often lead to a nutritional solution since nutrition affects every way the body works. The body cannot function properly without the right nutrients. Looking for the underlying cause takes a knowledge and understanding of how the body works beyond obvious symptoms. I believe that finding the underlying cause of a problem and fixing it is the only way to achieve long-term results. That's why understanding nutrition is extremely important to help improve a child's attention and behavior and to improve health.

The FDA restricts information on labels for nutrients. The labels can state how a nutrient can enhance good health but cannot reveal if the nutrient helps or cures a disease. For instance, a label on a particular nutrient can state that it supports a strong immune system but it cannot state that the nutrient will help with a disease such as a cold or flu unless the FDA has approved it for that disease. The FDA has approved Folic acid to prevent spina bifida, so this claim can be made.

Even though certain nutrients have been reported to be helpful, such as vitamin B6 which was found to be more effective then methylphenadate (Ritalin®) in double blind studies, no claim can be made that Vitamin B6 can treat ADHD on its label. The FDA considers ADHD to be a disease even though it was made up by the psychiatrists. Nutritional labels can seem rather vague unless you are familiar with the benefits and properties of nutrients.

NUTRITION 101 FOR PARENTS

We were taught in medical school that specific nutrients are needed in our body to make the biochemical processes work properly. There are literally hundreds of articles in the medical literature showing a correlation between certain nutritional deficiencies and many different health problems, from heart attacks to cancer. In addition, there are blood tests available to help identify nutritional deficiencies that I have found useful for my patients. Our bodies depend on nutrients to function. If we don't get enough of the right nutrients, our bodies can't work appropriately. You might not feel sick without these nutrients, but you may not actually be well either. Your body must compensate and work harder if you don't get the nutrients your body needs to maintain health.

THE AMERICAN DIET

Let's consider a typical school lunch. It often consists of a soda, chips and sweet desserts. Many schools even have soda and candy machines in the schools and actually encourage children to purchase these products because it brings in revenue to the school. With this kind of food and drink being provided in our schools, it is no wonder that our children are having problems.

There was a very interesting study done in 803 New York public schools and in nine juvenile correction facilities. In this study, researchers increased fruits and vegetables and whole grains and decreased fat and sugars. They then followed these children for a couple of years. They made no other changes in the schools and correctional facilities during that time period, thereby assuring the accuracy of the results, which were dramatic and astounding. After making these simple changes to the children's diets, the academic performance of 1.1 million children rose 16 % and learning disabilities fell 40%. In the juvenile correction facilities violent and non-violent antisocial behavior fell 48%. According to one of the researchers, the schools have not instituted any of these dietary changes on a permanent basis. Instead, the children in New York and the rest of the nation continue to be prescribed drugs. And when parents refuse to drug the children, those parents may be turned in to authorities for medical negligence. The negligence here is not with the parents. No child should be drugged in a school that promotes the sale of soft drinks and junk food.

DIET IS NOT ENOUGH

Even when we eat more nutritious foods, I do not believe

that we can get enough of the nutrients we need from our diets. Not only are most foods laden with sugar and artificial ingredients, many have chemicals added to lengthen their shelf life. Animals are fed antibiotics, hormones and other chemicals before they are slaughtered and fruits and vegetables are sprayed with pesticides while they are growing. All of these things can affect the quality of the foods we eat as well as add unhealthy toxins to our biological systems. Our environment also adds to our toxic load.

The pollution in our atmosphere and the toxins in our foods mean that our bodies have to work even harder to dispose of these toxic chemical by-products. For the liver to detoxify the toxins that enter our bodies, it must have the help of nutrients. The vitamins and minerals are used to make our biochemical processes work. Without an adequate supply of nutrients, our body simply cannot function properly. Many children diagnosed with the symptoms of ADHD show reactions and sensitivities to these food-based chemicals and environmental pollutants. They may also be deficient in many of the needed nutrients. That is why I recommend that my patients, as often as possible, eat organic and natural foods and take oral nutritional supplements.

In light of the many problems and concerns with the American diet, I believe that supplementing nutrients can help to make our children healthier, and, as I've seen in my practice, the supplements can make a major difference in how they feel and act. That's why I recommend supplements for all my patients. I have had children in my practice do nothing more than take supplements and improve significantly.

SUPPLEMENTS 101 FOR PARENTS

There has been much research on the effects of nutrients on behavior and attention. The following are the ones I find most beneficial for my patients. Remember, just because a nutrient is good for you, more of it is not necessarily better. While most nutrients have no known toxicity or side effects, some do have side effects in large doses. Do not exceed recommended doses. Locate a physician in your area who knows about nutrition and check with that physician before taking anything. Here is a list of specific nutrients and supportive literature.

Vitamin B6: Vitamin B6, in a double blind, crossover study published in *Biological Psychiatry* 1979 (14) 5, was found to be more effective than methylphenidate (Ritalin®) in a group of hyperactive children.

Thiamin: According to the *American Journal of Clinical Nutrition*, 1980 (33) 2, when thiamin deficiency was corrected, behavior improved.

Calcium: Supplementing calcium to deficient children may improve their hyperactivity (*Journal of Learning Disabilities*, 1975 (8): 354.

Magnesium: Magnesium deficiency in children is characterized by excessive fidgeting, anxious restlessness, psychomotor instability and learning difficulties in the presence of normal IQ. (*Magnesium in Health and Disease*, Seelig, Mildred, 1980) Magnesium is needed in more than 350 different biochemical reactions.

My own experiences with magnesium match those published in "Clinical Aspects of Chronic Magnesium Deficiency" (Seelig, Mildred, *Magnesium in Health and Disease*, Spectrum Publishing, 1980.) One teenage patient of mine said he felt dramatically better, calmer and better able to focus on his schoolwork when I treated him for his magnesium deficiency. Unfortunately, the typical American diet does not supply much magnesium. It is found in green leafy vegetables and nuts like cashews and almonds, which are not mainstays of most children's diet.

Vitamin C: When Vitamin C was increased by 50% it was found that IQ scores went up 3.6 points. (Kabula, A., *Journal of General Psychology*, 1960 (96) 343-352.) [It is thought that IQ is not supposed to change over one's lifetime, yet 3.6 points is a significant amount. The increase of 50% is equal to someone who was taking just 100 mg of Vitamin C increasing to 150 mg of Vitamin C.]

Niacin: Another B vitamin, was found to be helpful for the symptoms of hyperactivity, poor school performance, perceptual changes and inability to maintain social relationships. (Hoffer A., "Vitamin B3 dependent child." *Schizophrenia,* 1971 (3) 107-113.) [These are symptoms which many children who have received the ADHD label have in common.]

Pyridoxine, folic acid, thiamin, niacin, and vitamin C were the nutrients most commonly found to be low in children who measureably improved on supplementation. Deficiencies of vitamins A, E, B12, pantothenic acid, riboflavin, and other vitamins and minerals also were linked to bad behavior. Improvement could not be expected unless all deficiencies were corrected. (Schoenthaler, S.J., "Nutritional deficiencies and behavior" quoted in Bellanti J.A., Crook W.G., Layton R.E., eds. *Attention Deficit Hyperactivity Disorder: Causes and Possible Solutions.*

(Proceedings of a Conference). Jackson, TN: International Health Foundation, 1999.)

Zinc: Children with Zinc deficiencies were found to be irritable, tearful and sullen. They are not soothed by close body contact and resent disturbances. Zinc deficiencies result in hyperactivity and changes in seratonin levels. [Remember the SSRI drugs, Zoloft, Luvox, Paxil, Prozac, etc., that I mentioned in Step 1? These drugs are supposed to affect the seratonin levels in the body. Maybe the people who are taking these drugs are just Zinc deficient?] Not surprisingly, one study showed Zinc levels in children diagnosed with ADHD were found to be significantly lower than control (*Biological Psychiatry*, 1996).

DMAE: DMAE is a neurotransmitter precursor that has been used for years to improve behaviors, mental concentration, puzzle-solving ability and organization. DMAE was found to increase mental concentration after six weeks of use. This report was in the *Journal of Pediatrics* in 1958. [Pediatricians have had this information available to them for more than 40 years. Parents deserve to know about this information. One parent reported to me that her son's teacher thought that he had started taking Ritalin® when he had actually begun taking DMAE.]

Essential Fatty Acids (EFA's): Lower levels of Omega-3 Fatty Acids, which are found in fish oils and flax seed, were discovered in children who had more temper tantrums and sleep problems. (Stevens L.J., Zentall S.S., Deck J.L., Abate M.L., Watkins B.A., Lipp S.R., Burgess J. R. "Essential fatty acid metabolism in boys with attention-deficit hyperactivity disorder." (*American Journal of Clinical Nutrition*, 1995 (62) 4: 761-8.)

DHA, another EFA, is found in the central nervous system. High levels of DHA are important for learning, for visual function and for general central nervous system development. (Ensein, M., et al., *LIPIDS*, 1991 (26) 3.)

Deficiencies in the omega-3 fatty acids and DHA can impair learning. In addition, a significant number of boys with heath and learning problems were found to have lower total essential fatty acids. (Mitchell, E.A., et al, *Clinical Pediatrics*, 1987 (28) 8: 406-11.)

DHA is an Omega-3 Fatty Acid that is necessary for brain development and functioning. (Simopolos, A.P., "Omega-3 fatty acids in health and disease and in growth and development. " *American Journal of Clinical Nutrition* 1991, (54) 3:438-63)

l-Glutamine is an amino acid (a protein building block) and is important in supplying energy to the brain. It is also a brain neurotransmitter. It has been used to help curb sugar cravings, increase mental acuity, and to nutritionally support the nervous system. (Hackman, R.M. "Glutamine and Human Performance, *Nutrition Science,* March ,1997.)

Vitamin B$_{12}$ helps cells in the body grow and maintain normal function. It is an important vitamin for the nervous system. Vitamin B$_{12}$ is used to improve neurologic symptoms such as loss of memory and moodiness. (*American Journal of Clinical Nutrition,* 16 January 2001 (71): 514-522.)

Chromium is an essential trace mineral. Low chromium levels may be a contributing factor of hypoglycemia in some people. (Anderson, R.A., Polansky, M.M., Bryden, N.A., Bhathena, S.J., Canary, J.J. "Effects of supplemental chromium on patients with symptoms of reactive hypoglycemia," *Metabolism,* 1987 (36): 351–355.)

Figure 9

Daily Recommendation
Always check with your physician before using.

Age	4-6	7-11	12 and up
Vitamin A (as beta carotene)	3500 IU	7000 IU	10,500 IU
Vitamin E (IU)	100 IU	200 IU	300-800 IU
Vitamin B1, Thiamine	1 5 mg	10 mg	15 mg
B2	5 mg	10 mg	15 mg
Niacin	15 mg	30 mg	45 mg
B6	10 mcg	20 mcg	30 mcg
Folic Acid	400 mcg	800 mcg	1200 mcg
Vitamin B12	20 mcg	40 mcg	60 mcg
Pantothenic Acid	25 mg	50 mg	75 mg
Calcium	100 mg	200 mg	300 mg
Magnesium	150 mg	300 mg	450 mg
Zinc	5 mg	10 mg	15 mg
Chromium	30 mcg	60 mcg	90 mcg
L-Glutamine	1500 mg	3000 mg	4500 mg
Flax Meal	500 mg	1000 mg	1500 mg
Vitamin C	250 mg	500 mg	1000 mg
Evening Primrose Oil	500 mg	500 mg	500 mg
DHA	100 mg	100 mg	100 mg
DMAE (By Weight)	<75 lbs.	75-125 lbs.	125 lbs. +
	100 mg	150 mg	200 mg

Step 4—Take Your A, B, C's, Vitamins, That Is

Remember:

- Nutrients are needed for the body to work properly.

- I recommend supplements for all my patients.

- Some nutrients have been shown to have a positive effect on behavior and attention.

STEP 5—ATTACK THE ALLERGIES

Allergies do affect how we think, feel and act. Conventional allergists have told me and many of my patients this is not so. They were taught that allergies do not affect behavior or learning. The medical literature says otherwise. The *Annals of Allergy*, one of the top medical journals on allergies, reported the following in a 1993 issue. [*See Figure 10*.]

The report says the "coincidence of the pollen season, with the timing of examinations, discriminates unfairly against children suffering from allergies. It further asserts that unless the children's allergies can be effectively treated, they should not be expected to maintain the same rate of learning as their normal peers and that it would be fair and/or wise to postpone examinations until the pollen season has passed. "

Of course, the recommendations from this report are not being implemented in schools. Instead, these children are being placed on amphetamine-like drugs such as Ritalin® and Adderall for what could be an undiagnosed and untreated allergy. I see this all the time in my practice. I find that children who have been on these drugs or whose parents have been pressured to put their child on one of these drugs actually have allergies that caused the learning and behavior symptoms.

Figure 10

Seasonal Allergic Rhinitis and Antihistamine Effects
on Children's Learning
Annals of Allergy, 1993
(Summary)

1. Seasonal allergic rhinitis afflicts up to 10% of school chil-
    dren and 21-30% of adolescents. Absences from school and
    poor performances while attending school are deemed to
    be among the most serious personal and societal conse-
    quences of the disease.
2. Children attending school while symptomatic are often de-
    scribed as apathetic, absent-minded and disinterested in
    educational and social activities.
3. The atopic (allergic) child was significantly less knowledge-
    able than normal controls.
4. The normal child's average learning performance was in
    every way superior to the allergic child's, no matter how the
    latter had been treated before instructions.
5. From this we conclude that seasonal allergic rhinitis, by
    itself, can cause learning impairment.
6. The usual coincidence of the pollen season with prepara-
    tion for end-term examinations discriminates unfairly
    against children suffering from the effects of seasonal aller-
    gic rhinitis.
7. Unless those children's disorder can be effectively treated,
    allowing them to maintain the same rate of learning as
    their normal peers it would be fair and wise to postpone
    crucial tutoring and examinations until the pollen season
    has passed.

ALLERGY TESTING

In my office, during allergy testing, I have seen dramatic
evidence of how allergies affect learning. I use the child's
medical history and food preferences to help decide which

substances to allergy test. The child is then given one drop of a food or inhalent allergen in the skin by injection with a very small needle. These are given at 10-minute intervals to see if the child reacts. Even children who are initially very scared of getting allergy tested find that the shots hurt very little or not at all. Most children actually enjoy the experience once their initial concerns about getting shots are overcome.

ONE AT A TIME

There are two different ways to do skin testing. One method is to test all the allergens at one time by placing a drop of the allergen under the skin on the arm or the back. With this test, the doctor is looking for the reaction to the allergen on the skin. The skin may turn red or grow a red, irritated skin blister (wheal). The other is to test for one allergen at a time. I prefer the second method. During each 10-minute interval the patient can be monitored for any changes in heart rate, breathing capacity, behavior, concentration and small motor skills, as well as the possibility of a skin reaction. In addition, many children with the symptoms of ADHD have a history of asthma, which can be incited during testing.

By testing the allergies one at a time, we can observe which allergens are underlying the asthma symptoms and any attention or behavior symptoms. Typical allergic symptoms like runny nose, watery eyes and headaches can also occur. To look for the different possible reactions to each specific antigen is, in my opinion, very important because each child may react differently. If the testing is done all at once, a finding could be missed. If all of the allergens are placed on the skin at one time and a reaction occurs other than a skin reaction, no one would know which allergen was causing which symptom. When the allergens are tested one at a time, it is usually quite clear which allergen is causing it. When patients know what type of symptoms an allergen causes, they can decide the best form of treatment.

UNCOVERING LEARNING DIFFICULTIES

During each testing interval, the child is asked to write his/her name and do some concentration work such as reading. One patient, Mike, who was five years old when he was tested, could print his name very well before we started, but as we tested him for apple, there were major changes in his handwriting. His behavior was also changing. Mike's writing samples done during allergy testing can be seen in Figure 11. It shows the effect apple has on his handwriting. At the top right of the page you can see Mike's pretesting signature. What follows is Mike's handwriting samples as they correlate with the testing of different dilutions of the allergen, apple. As you can see, Mike lost control of his ability to write correctly. He began scribbling and writing backwards. Mike's behavior also worsened at the same time. The final dose, a weaker dose of the allergen apple, is the dose that brought Mike's handwriting and his behavior back to normal. Now, Mike's parents know the effect apple has on Mike's behavior and on his ability to write, to concentrate and to learn. Mike's parents can remove apple from his diet or he can take an allergy injection of the dose of the apple allergen that cleared up his handwriting and his behavior symptoms. He can then eat apple without the negative effect.

A PICTURE IS WORTH A THOUSAND WORDS

In my speaking engagements and at legislative hearings I

Step 5—Attack the Allergies

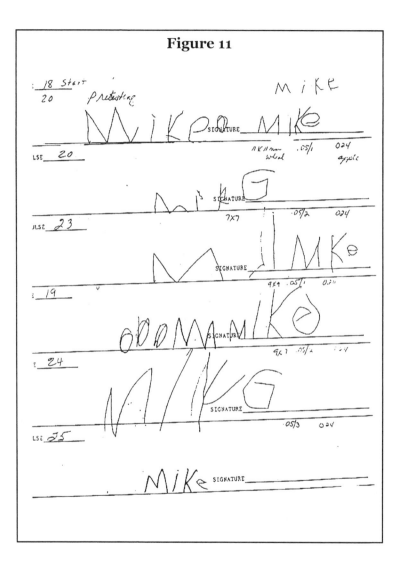

Figure 11

do around the country, I show a videotape of a young patient being tested at The Block Center. This child's reactions to the antigen are typical of the symptoms psychiatry calls ADHD. The video is a powerful and compelling example of how the symptoms can be a result of an allergic reaction. It is included in the video of my seminar, *The Road To No More Ritalin*®. This is what the video shows. Nine-year-old Wesley, right before he is given a testing dose of chocolate, is sweet and delightful. He is asked how he is feeling to which he replies, "fine." He appears relaxed and comfortable. He is then given a small dose of the allergy extract, chocolate, under his skin. During each ten-minute testing cycle, we ask the children to do the five minutes of concentration work to see if they are able to concentrate after the shot. Wesley cannot. Within minutes after receiving this dose of chocolate, his personality changes. He is angry, frustrated, and easily agitated. He yells at his mother, pounds the desk and stomps his feet. He is unable to sit still and concentrate. When we find the right dose of the allergy extract, Wesley's adverse symptoms stop. He is like a completely different child. He becomes very cooperative. He can sit still, concentrate and get his work done. I see this kind of reaction everyday in my office.

Watching this video of a child reacting to a specific substance shows how important allergies can be in influencing how our children think, feel, and act. The problem is not always chocolate. It could have been any food or anything in the air. It is different with each child. Usually there is more than just one allergen involved. Wesley reacted like this to several different allergens.

Step 5—Attack the Allergies

ALLERGIES, SENSITIVITIES AND TESTING

So many parents come to my office and tell me that their child has already tested negative for allergies. Their allergist has told them that their child has no food allergies and that allergies in general do not cause behavior and attention problems. I usually find very different results. Perhaps this is because I am using a different testing method.

There are many studies in the medical literature that show that there is an association between foods and behavior. There is also a correlation between exposures to various chemicals and nervous system reactions such as headaches, mental fuzziness and difficulty focusing.

TOP CAUSES OF ALLERGY SYMPTOMS

When parents know what to look for when it comes to allergies, it can be very helpful in the search for answers to their child's health and learning problems. A child can feel better very quickly when the foods or environmental irritants are identified and removed. Although I have found that some children are highly sensitive to lettuce or orange juice, these tend to be specific and unique to them. Just like Wesley had a specific sensitivity reaction to chocolate, other children may have some very specific foods or chemicals that affect only them. However, I have generally found that certain foods and substances cause some degree of problems in the vast majority of my patients.

GOT MILK? MAYBE NOT!

The number one food allergen I find in my patients with

behavior and learning problems is cow's milk. Many of these children will improve to some degree when milk is removed from their diet. Parents tell me it is fairly easy to remove milk because there are so many good-tasting options available today such as soymilk and rice milk.

I have many children in my practice who have been my patients since they were born. I have recommended that the mothers breast feed them for at least one year and to keep cow's milk out of their diets completely even after they have stopped nursing. All of these babies have been remarkably healthy. At worst, they have had colds and occasional fluid in the ears. I don't believe a single one of them needed antibiotics in at least the first two or three years of life that I have worked with them. This is a sharp contrast to other children I have seen who have a great deal of dairy in their diets. The breast-feeding is certainly immune protective, but I have seen many children who were breast-fed but later put a significant amount of dairy into their diets. Many of these children have had asthma, ear infections, respiratory infections and/or behavior problems. If a child has allergies, they are more likely to have problems in school. The performance of children with allergies was inferior to children without allergies in all areas. It is so important to consider allergies as part of the problem.

In my practice, it has been helpful to adjust infant feeding to prevent food allergy reactions. If a parent does not nurse and uses formula instead, I recommend that they use four different bases such as soy, rice and hypoallergenic formulas which are rotated every four days to lessen the baby's chances of developing a sensitivity to any of them. I always counsel avoidance of cow's milk.

Step 5—Attack the Allergies

Doctors are taught to wait until an infant is at least nine months old to introduce cow's milk and other proteins into an infant's diet because their digestive systems are not prepared to break down these types of foods so early in their development. Yet doctors do not think twice about starting a non-nursed baby on formula containing cow's milk, even at one day old. Cow's milk may be the perfect mother's milk for a calf, but it certainly is not perfect for a human baby. I believe this early introduction of cow's milk into the diet causes infants to develop an allergic reaction to the milk's proteins. Then as the child get older, they remain allergic or sensitive to milk. The fact that most children are given milk at such an early age probably explains why milk is the number one food allergen I find in my practice. Many parents report improvement in many different symptoms when milk is removed.

AND THE LIST GOES ON

The next most common allergen I find, wheat, includes breads, pastas, and cereals -- not just "whole wheat" products but white bread, too. Wheat and milk can be the source of chronic ear infections. I discuss this in more detail in my video, *Treating Ear and Respiratory Infections WITHOUT Antibiotics*. In one study, researchers found that one-third of children with ear fluid were allergic to milk and one-third to wheat. Those who avoided the allergic foods had significant reduction of the fluid in the ears. When the allergic foods were added back into the diets, more than 94% had clogged middle ears again within 4 months.

Ear infections are a very common chronic health problem in babies. I find that the main underlying cause of these infections is allergies. As children get older these allergies manifest in different ways, provoking different symptoms. Very often I see behavior and learning problems as a result.

If wheat is removed from a child's diet, there are many other grains and flours such as rice, spelt, soy, and millet that are abundantly available at health food stores. These can be purchased in packages for baking or as ready made and packaged pastas, breads, cookies, and many other common foods.

Other foods to which I often see reactions are corn, yeast, orange, soy, peanut, baker's yeast, beef and chicken. It is important to read all food labels to check that none of the offending foods are in the product. Manufacturers change their recipes from time to time so it's a good idea to read the label every time a product is purchased.

AIRBORNE ALLERGIES

There are other culprits to consider like inhalants such as trees, weeds, grass, mold, cat, dog, dust and dust mites. These are the irritants we think of when we hear the term allergy. They can be a problem and do need to be addressed. Children with chronic respiratory allergies may feel like they have a head cold everyday. You know how difficult it is to think and to learn when you have a respiratory infection. No wonder these children with airborne allergies have problems learning in school.

CHEMICAL SENSITIVITIES

When an advertisement for a fragrance says it's like a spring garden, that's because it's been formulated to smell like a spring garden. It is not a spring garden. Many of these chemical fragrances are made from petroleum chemicals. We spray these substances in the air, heat them up in our electrical outlets, and apply them to our bodies through soaps, creams and perfumes. Can you imagine going to the gas station, squeezing the nozzle, filling your cupped hand with gasoline and splashing it all over your body? Not a very pleasant thought, is it? Can you also imagine filling a spray bottle with the gasoline and going home and spraying your house with it? That is what you might be doing when you use some of these products. No wonder our children do not feel well. And for people with asthma, it's worse. One study found that 95% of asthmatics start wheezing when they are exposed to fragrances. I always recommend that my patients never wear or use fragrances. Even if it doesn't bother them, it could cause a serious health problem for someone with asthma or other bronchial problems.

RAID AND DISCARD INSECTICIDES

Insecticide products present another chemical problem that affect our children and should never be used in the home. I know we've all been told that these toxins are safe and are only dangerous to the insects. If that were true, the government would not have banned similar poisons in the past despite previous assurances of safety. So which insecticides, currently being called "safe" today, will be pulled off the shelves tomorrow? It is a "buyer beware" marketplace where chemicals are concerned. The problem is that all too often the negative effects of these products are revealed after they have been in our homes and in our environment for a long time and after they have caused problems.

Insecticides are poisons. They kill the insects by affecting their nervous systems. Children, with developing nervous systems, are more susceptible and vulnerable to the effects of insecticides and there is no need to expose them to these toxic chemicals. There are books available on the market today that provide many effective and safer alternatives to insecticides.

NO SMOKING

I will not see a child at my center if a parent smokes. The parent should never smoke in any of the air space the child uses, even when the child is not in the space at the time. That means never smoke in the car if the child is _ever_ a passenger in that car and never smoke in the house. This also means to never allow anyone else to smoke in those spaces or around your child. I cannot emphasize this enough. Smoke is a very serious toxin and it causes as many health risks for the non-smoker as for the smoker. Smoke clings to the walls and permeates everything in the space and stays long after the cigarette, cigar, or pipe is out. Aside from the obvious health problems — lung cancer, emphysema, chronic bronchitis and heart disease — the chemicals in tobacco smoke have been documented to cause the symptoms we think of as ADHD. One patient did not believe that her cigarette smoke influenced her child's behavior. When I allergy tested her child for tobacco smoke, his behavior changed dramatically. That mom never picked up another cigarette after seeing what a major negative effect it had on her child's behavior.

DISCOUNTING THE PATIENT

There are many chemicals in our environment with new ones being added all the time. We are just beginning to understand the affect these chemicals have on our environment and on our bodies. I see health problems resulting from chemical exposure everyday. These are not the acute exposures that send people to the emergency room but the chronic ones that cause a multitude of baffling symptoms such as behavior and learning problems, headaches, tiredness, muscle and joint pain and other chronic problems.

Too many doctors fall back on what I call "The Coincidence Excuse." Physicians know that it is very common for children labeled with ADHD to also have allergies. One doctor I know who considers himself to be an expert in the field of ADHD has been quoted as saying that this association between ADHD symptoms and allergy is simply a coincidence. This physician would rather label his patients with the psychiatric diagnosis of ADHD and drug them than open his mind and take the time to find out what is really causing the problem.

HOW TO LOOK FOR FOOD ALLERGIES/ SENSITIVITIES

Food allergies and sensitivities can be evaluated at home through a system called The Elimination-Challenge Diet. I find the foods the child loves the most and is least likely to want to give up are the ones most likely to be causing the problems. The parent selects one of those foods, especially one that a child is eating everyday. That food is completely eliminated for five to seven days. The food must be <u>completely</u> eliminated for the test to be valid, which means all labels must be read very carefully to be sure the eliminated food is not hiding in other foods the child eats. This is a very common error.

Step 5—Attack the Allergies

Eliminating a child's favorite foods may not be easy because it will probably be missed. But if the food is completely eliminated, the child's behavior may improve by the fourth or fifth day. After two consecutive "good" days, the challenge part of the diet begins. If "good" days do not occur, there are probably other foods which will need to be eliminated or the child may have airborne allergies to such things as trees, weeds, molds, and dust. A physician who tests allergens one at a time could be helpful at this point.

After eliminating the food for five to seven days, and seeing an improvement in symptoms, the child may eat the foods again but under very specific guidelines. Only one eliminated food can be introduced each day on an empty stomach. Signs and symptoms may then be observed. Food symptoms can be much more dramatic and obvious when the food has been cleared out of the system.

The reaction can be physical (runny nose, wheezing, cough, stomach gas, stomach cramps, headache) or emotional (anger, anxiety, agitation, nervousness, hyperactivity). The reaction can occur immediately or it may take several hours. If a reaction occurs, the child must not eat that food again. If the reaction is severe, the child's symptoms may improve with the use of Alka Seltzer Gold (Alka Seltzer in the orange box), one tablet for children under age 12 and two for twelve and older. The tablet is dissolved in a cup of water and the child sips it. Alka Seltzer Gold is the same as regular Alka Seltzer but contains no aspirin. It will sometimes neutralize a food sensitivity reaction. If the child does not react to the food, the food is considered to be safe and the child can continue to eat it. The child may eat other foods that have not been removed from the diet during this time.

Step 5—Attack the Allergies

The next day another food can be challenged in the same manner. If the child is still reacting from the previous day, the challenge of the next food must be postponed until the reaction has stopped. This is repeated each day until all foods have been challenged.

QUICK TIPS FOR FOOD REACTIONS

If a child eats an offending food and begins to show signs of a reaction, there are a few quick tips that can be tried immediately to help alleviate or to stop the reaction. [*See Figure 12.*]

Figure 12
Helpful Hints After a Food Reaction Occurs

1. Alka Seltzer Gold (in orange box) one tablet age 6-12, 2 tablets 12 or over. Dissolve in water, add ice and sip.
2. Vitamin C to bowel tolerance. This is to increase bowel emptying so that offending food will leave the system more quickly. Age 6-12, 250 mg/hour, age 12 and older, 500-1000 mg/hour until loose stools develop.
3. Activated charcoal. Follow directions on bottle. This is a black powder and can be very messy.

WARNING
An IgE food reaction can cause hives or throat constriction which can be life-threatening. If a child has eaten a food at least twice and had no serious reactions, it is unlikely to occur in an elimination-challenge diet. However, if a child has a history of asthma, the asthma could worsen with the challenge. A doctor should always be consulted before trying any of these suggestions.

OTHER TESTING METHODS

A second way to evaluate food allergies and sensitivities is to do a blood test, called a RAST test that can determine through the blood the presence of an IgE allergy to a food. An IgE reaction causes an immediate reaction such as hives, itching, or breathing difficulties. While blood tests can tell if someone is allergic or sensitive to certain foods, they will not tell what kind of reaction someone has to that food. Neither will it indicate the appropriate dose for treatment. The only choice for treatment from blood test results is elimination. The third method of looking for allergies and sensitivities is with skin testing.

WHAT TO DO?

If a child tests as allergic to specific foods, there are several options. The foods can be completely eliminated from a child's diet. I have heard children as young as four years old say that they never want to eat their favorite food again after they realized how bad it made them feel and act. This option works well unless the food is hidden in many other foods and is difficult to avoid or if the child is allergic or sensitive to so many other foods that as a practical matter they cannot all be removed. Most of the parents I see in my office choose the antigen shots because they work quickly and are more convenient than changing the diet. Once the proper dose is established, the parents can give their child the shots at home. There is one other method that parents can do at home and it too is an effective approach, The Rotation Diet, which I will explain step by step.

Step 5—Attack the Allergies

THE FOUR-DAY ROTATION DIET

The following information is from the Rotation Diet Plan I developed. Although my program includes a magnetic food planner and video instruction, this reprint of the instructions is complete.

A four-day rotation period is used because food normally passes through the body's digestive system within that period. If a food is eaten again while the body still has any part of that food in the system, an individual is more likely to develop sensitivity to that food. For this reason, while on the Rotation Diet, no single food should be eaten more frequently than every fourth day. For instance, if chicken is eaten on Monday, it is not eaten again until Friday. Foods from the same food family may be eaten every other day. For example, wheat and corn are in the same food family. Wheat may be eaten on Monday, corn on Wednesday and wheat again on Friday.

In the diet, foods are grouped by "families" based on the <u>source</u> of the ingredients and by "type" of food from that source.

> *EXAMPLE: grass is the family for wheat (a food type) and corn (another food type)*

Here's how it works.
- To properly rotate, food intake from any food type is limited to once every four days.
- The different food types from the same food family can be eaten every other day.
- A day's food intake may include as many portions of the food type as is appropriate for good nutrition, but foods from that type should <u>not</u> be consumed the following day, and the same food

should <u>not</u> be consumed for at least four days.

EXAMPLE:
Rotating the Grass Family (Wheat and Corn, etc.):

> *Two common grains, wheat and corn, are grouped together in the grass family of foods. A rotation diet permits consumption of wheat once in four days and corn once in four days. Rotate foods to avoid consuming food from the same food family two days in a row. They may be consumed in the following rotation:*

Monday:	*Wheat*
Tuesday:	
Wednesday:	*Corn*
Thursday:	
Friday:	*Wheat*
Saturday:	
Sunday:	*Corn*

MEAL PLANNING WITH A ROTATION DIET

First:

- Meal planning begins by listing the foods the family likes and finds convenient to prepare.
- List standard foods served for meals throughout the day, including breakfast, lunch, dinner and snack foods.
- List the ingredients for each food, noting both the <u>primary ingredients</u> (<u>wheat</u> pasta in spaghetti, <u>corn</u> tortillas in enchiladas) and the secondary ingredients (tomato, garlic, onion, <u>corn</u> oil and oregano for spaghetti sauce; to-

mato, cheese, onion and chili powder for enchiladas).

- Notice which components fall into the same food families. In the example above, wheat and corn fall into the grass family. Rotation planning requires that these foods be served at least one day apart, and that wheat pasta not be served more than once in four days. The list of favorite foods would lead to a plan with pasta or any other form of wheat as an available component of dishes no more frequently than once every four days.

It will still be necessary to eliminate completely any food that causes a severe allergic reaction.

Figure 13 lists the Biological Classification of Foods and Food Families. If only one food is represented in a food family, that food is listed alone. For example, tuna, chocolate and banana are listed singly. These may be eaten every four days without regard to the consumption of other foods. Food types from the same family can be scheduled all on the same day or in other combinations, *as long as the same food is not repeated more often than every four days or food families more often than every two days.*

Once a rotation diet plan has been selected, a copy should be made on a sheet of paper and used for grocery shopping trips. A sample week of foods based on the rotation diet follows:

Monday: tuna, pork, broccoli, mushroom, cantaloupe, grapes, wheat, rice, cashews, rice syrup, grape juice, cashew milk, baker's yeast, sunflower oil

Tuesday: chicken, eggs, shrimp, onion, carrot, banana, pear, soy flour, almonds, beet sugar, pear juice, almond milk, garlic, carob, soy oil

Wednesday: turkey, sole, lettuce, cucumber, orange, mango, olives, corn, oats, pistachios, cane sugar, corn syrup, clove, cocoa, olive oil, corn oil

Thursday: beef, cheese, tomato, potato, apple, buckwheat, walnuts, maple syrup, apple juice, tomato juice, cayenne, chili powder, basil, butter

Friday: Same as Monday

Saturday: Same as Tuesday

Sunday: Same as Wednesday

EFFORT VS. BENEFIT

If a child is totally out of control because of a reaction to food, it might be a lot less effort to change the diet than it is to deal with the behavioral symptoms. Although it takes a great deal of effort to set up the diet, like any change, it will become easier and more natural as time goes by. If a child's behavior improves then life will become easier as well. I have found that the parents who come to my office are willing to do whatever it takes to help their children.

Many doctors do not provide patients with the option of changing the child's diet. Doctors have told me they believe a modified diet could be helpful but is too difficult. One actually said he was aware food reactions could affect

Figure 13
Biological Classification of Foods and Food Families

Fungi: baker's yeast, brewer's yeast, mushroom

Grass: barley, corn, millet, oat, rice, rye, sugar, wheat, spelt, wild rice

Palm: coconut, date,

Lily: asparagus, chives, garlic, leek, onion, shallot, aloe vera

Banana: banana, plantain, arrowroot

Walnut: walnut, pecan, butternut, hickory nut

Buckwheat

Pineapple

Goosefoot: beet, spinach, sugar beet, quinoa

Nutmeg: nutmeg, mace

Laurel: avocado, bay leaf, cinnamon

Mustard: broccoli, brussel sprouts, cabbage, cauliflower, collards, horseradish, kale, mustard greens, radish, turnip, watercress

Rose: apple, pear, almond, apricot, cherry, nectarine, peach, plum, blackberry, boysenberry, raspberry, strawberry

Legume: black beans, black-eyed peas, carob, fava beans, garbanzo beans, green beans, kidney beans, lentil, licorice, lima beans, navy beans, pea, peanut, soy

Citrus: grapefruit, lemon, lime, orange, tangerine

Cashew: cashew, mango, pistachio

Maple

Grape: cream of tartar, raisen, grape, wine, wine vinegar

Figure 13—Cont'd.

Chocolate: cocoa, chocolate
Carrot: carrot, celery, cumin, dill, parsley
Heath: blueberry, cranberry
Mint: basil, marjoram, oregano, peppermint, rosemary,
     sage, thyme
Potato: eggplant, pepper, potato, tomato
Gourd: cucumber, melons, pumpkin, squashes
Composite: lettuce, safflower, sunflower seed, tarragon
Mollusk: clam, oyster, scallop, mussel
Crustacean: crab, crayfish, lobster, prawn, shrimp
Codfish: cod, haddock, pollack whiting
Catfish
Dolphin: mahi-mahi
Mackeral: albacore, mackeral, tuna
Flounder: flounder, halibut, sole, turbot
Snapper
Salmon: salmon, trout species
Whitefish
Bass: white perch, yellow bass
Duck: duck, goose
Pheasant: chicken/eggs, pheasant, quail, cornish hen
Turkey
Swine: pork (bacon, ham, sausage)
Deer: deer, elk, moose
Beef: beef (gelatin, cow's milk products, cheese), veal,
     buffalo, goat, lamb

Figure 14
4-Day Rotation Diet
Children's Counting Poem

I eat some of my favorite foods each day,
It's good for me in every way.
It makes me feel my very best,
I'm happy, calm and full of zest.
I eat spaghetti all day long,
And then I start my counting song.
Wait day 1, day, 2, day 3, day 4,
And then its time to eat some more.
While I'm counting the days, I still get to eat
My other favorite foods and treats.
This counting song made it easy to learn,
That all my foods must wait their turn.

---

behavior because his own child reacted adversely to chocolate. In spite of this, he does not inform his patients of this connection. No wonder so many children suffer with health and learning problems if even parents who are willing to put out the effort to change their child's diet don't receive support and information from their doctor. I understand; I have been a young mother out there alone searching for answers. It is hard, but it can be done.

Step 5—Attack the Allergies

Step 5—Attack the Allergies

Remember:

- Allergies effect how we feel, think, act and learn.
- Allergies can be uncovered through elimination challenge diet or skin testing one at a time.
- Milk is the number one food allergy.
- Remember the importance of:
    - No pesticides
    - No smoking
    - No fragrances

STEP 6 — REPAIR THE GUT

How well we are able to nourish our body fundamentally determines our health and well being. We depend on our digestive system to function well in order to help keep the body healthy. When the digestive system is ill, the whole body is ill. Just think how sick you feel when you have an acute stomach virus. Low intake of nutrients and fluids during the illness also has a negative affect on all other body systems. A host of subtle symptoms persist after the acute stage until the digestion and nutrition normalize and once again begin to fuel the body.

A chronic, low-grade gastric problem effects how you feel, think, and act on a daily basis. Many of my patients labeled with ADHD actually suffer with undiagnosed, chronic stomach problems which not only caused the attention and behavior symptoms but also interfered with normal digestion and optimal nutrition. Approximately 25% of my patients had parasites and most of them had never left the country; approximately 50% had pathological bacteria in their gut that required treatment, and about 90% had an overgrowth of yeast. There are several causes of these gastrointestinal problems.

LEAKY GUT SYNDROME

Leaky gut syndrome occurs when the mucus lining of the intestine or the "gut" actually "leaks" bacteria and under-digested food particles into the blood stream. Generally, during digestion, foods are broken down and converted into a smaller, usable form before being absorbed into the blood stream through small openings in the stomach lining. Bacteria and other by-products of digestion that do not belong in the blood steam move through the gut, without leaking out until they are expelled from the body through normal elimination. However, if the lining of the gut is inflamed or damaged in some way, the openings in the lining that serve as a protective barrier become more porous, allowing larger food particles and bacteria to "leak out." The body tags these particles as foreign invaders and produces antibodies to attack them. When the particles are foods, the body will then identify those foods as foreign and an allergic reaction results whenever that food is eaten.

Allergies can cause a variety of attention and behavior symptoms including mood swings, foggy thinking, aggression, sleepiness and hyperactivity. In addition, when the blood sends bacteria and larger food particles throughout the body, they settle in different places. When this occurs, the antibodies can inadvertently attack not only the particles but also the tissues into which they have settled which sets up a chronic inflammatory process. Autoimmune diseases such as Rheumatoid Arthritis, Crohn's disease and ulcerative colitis may be a result of Leaky Gut Syndrome if antibodies are attacking particles that have settled in the joints, nerves, and other organs.

All of the symptoms of these autoimmune illnesses also include serious stomach inflammation. Though the stomach symptoms are usually considered part of the disease, they actually could be the cause of the disease. The conventional thought is that the body is mysteriously attacking itself. I don't ascribe to that theory. Our body is designed to take care of itself and to heal itself, thus the importance of looking for and treating underlying problems. I try to find safe, rational methods to help the body to heal itself and to function at its optimal capacity rather than covering symptoms with drugs. With drugs, the patient will feel better briefly but the actual health problem has not been addressed and often the underlying problem will continue to progress.

CAUSES OF INFLAMMATION IN THE GUT OR "LEAKY GUT SYNDROME"

Researchers recently discovered elevations of the protein Zonulin, in the intestinal tracts of people with certain autoimmune disorders, which may be responsible for causing the lining of the intestine to become more permeable.

ANTIBIOTICS

The most common problem of the gut I see is an overgrowth of yeast caused by the misuse and overuse of antibiotics. Most of the children I see have been placed on multiple rounds of antibiotics for recurring respiratory and ear infections since an early age. Even though they are not taking antibiotics currently, the yeast overgrowth from the previous use is still present in the intestinal tract.

Oral antibiotics that help kill the bacteria causing ear or respiratory infections also kill off the "good" bacteria in the gut leaving room for yeast overgrowth. Antibiotics do not kill yeast. A single round of antibiotics can throw off the intestinal flora, or good bacteria, essential to break down food. Multiple rounds of antibiotics do not allow the gut to rebound but give the yeast more than ample time to take over.

WHAT IS CANDIDA?

Candida albicans, a fungus naturally present on the skin and in the gut, grows in the intestinal tract harmlessly in balance with the normal flora until that "friendly" bacteria is reduced, allowing the candida to grow unimpeded.

CANDIDA HEALTH PROBLEMS

Overgrowth of candida and other yeast can cause problems outside the gut such as vaginitis in women and thrush, a fungus coating of the mouth and throat, often found in infants. In the gut, candida overgrowth inflames the intestinal lining and may be one of the causes of Leaky Gut Syndrome and all its associative problems. In addition, the fungus releases wastes into the bloodstream that can have a negative effect on the nervous and immune systems.

A child who has had antibiotic treatment and who eats the usual sugar-laden diet is the perfect host for candida or yeast overgrowth. William Crook, MD, author of *The Yeast Connection,* reports helping many children with attention and behavior symptoms by treating digestive track yeast. I have found the same results.

CANDIDIASIS TREATMENTS

"Good" bacteria should be replaced during and after antibiotic treatment. I recommend daily doses of this good bacteria known as a probiotic to reverse or to prevent a yeast infection. Daily doses are also important because of the fragility of this "friendly" bacteria. Probiotics can be found in health food stores and should be refrigerated for preservation until consumed.

Probiotics, which comes in capsules or powder, have a neutral to sweet taste and in powder can be sprinkled over cereal or mixed in cold drinks without changing the taste. Although probiotics come in many different brands, the important consideration is to have at least 2.25 billion live organisms of Lactobacillus per serving. I usually recommend that my patients take a serving two to three times each day.

KILL OFF THE CANDIDA

The gut will not return to balance simply by replenishing the good bacteria. The yeast overgrowth must also be killed off via one of several excellent natural and prescription treatments. However, it is important to identify which will be most effective through a laboratory evaluation of the gut. I use special labs that evaluate the gut through stool samples that look for bacteria, yeast or parasites and also tests for sensitivity to various prescription and natural treatments. Some of the common treatments for yeast are Fluconazole, Ketoconazole, Itraconazole and Nystatin, all prescription drugs. Unfortunately, I have found that Nystatin, an older drug, is no longer as effective as new strains of yeast have developed resistance to it.

Certain natural substances have been found to be effective and when indicated would be my recommendation. They include: Berberine, Caprylic Acid, Garlic, Undecylenic Acid and Plant Tannins.

CHANGE THE DIET

Yeast can also be affected with dietary changes. Yeast lives off of carbohydrates such as bread, sugars, cookies, cakes, and sodas as well as mushrooms and yeast and mold from breads. The yeast diet eliminates such foods as sugars, sweets, and lactose-containing dairy products except for butter, thus starving the yeast.

It may be necessary to stay on this diet for several months or even longer to kill off all the yeast overgrowth. The time period may be shortened if implemented in combination with a natural or prescription treatment.

THE ANTI-YEAST DIET

The following foods are eliminated from the diet

1. Sugar in all forms, including honey.

2. Fungus, molds, and yeast

This will include commercially-baked goods, mushrooms, vinegar and all foods containing vinegar, including salad dressing, pickled vegetables, green olives, and sauerkraut. Fermented products which produce mold and fungus include apple cider, dry roasted nuts, barbecue potato chips, commercial soups, white flour, bacon and pork, soy sauce and tofu. Vitamins and minerals may have hidden yeast, especially many of the B vitamins. Other moldy foods include processed meats such as dried and smoked meat, sausage, hot dogs, luncheon meats, smoked turkey, and smoked salmon. Also, nuts and seeds will often contain mold.

3. All white grains. This includes white rice and pasta.

4. Potatoes and corn.

5. Herb teas and spices.

Foods that can be eaten on the Anti-Yeast Diet:

1. Eggs, fish, chicken, turkey, seafood, lamb, or veal

2. Vegetables

3. Salad greens that can be topped with vegetable oil and fresh lemon juice.

4. Brown rice and millet, whole grain or sprouted wheat bread or wholegrain pasta. Limit bread and pasta to two to three servings each day.

5. Whole fruit, not juice, two servings per day. Eat fruits at the time they are cut. After a fruit has been cut, it is more likely to grow mold.

When symptoms resolve, some foods can be slowly reintroduced. There is no need to add sugar back into the diet.

PREVENTION

Restricting foods that feed the yeast can help prevent growth. A healthy diet with limited complex carbohydrates and no sugar, which includes more proteins and vegetables, will help to prevent a return of the yeast. But in my opinion, antibiotic use remains the greatest cause of yeast overgrowth.

NO MORE ANTIBIOTICS

In my second book, *No More Antibiotics*, I explain the many problems with antibiotic use, including yeast overgrowth. Most of the children I see for attention and behavioral symptoms have had chronic ear and respiratory infections since they were very young. The common treatment has, of course, been antibiotics. Yet, researchers have found that the sooner these children with ear infections were given antibiotics, the longer the infections lasted and the more often they recurred. If the antibiotic was given on the first day of the infection, the frequency of recurrence was almost three times greater than those who received no antibiotics. If physicians waited at least eight days before prescribing the antibiotics, the ear infections resolved as quickly as in the children who had been given no antibiotics. Medical literature indicates that 80 to 90% of all ear infections will heal entirely on their own. Clearly, treating ear infections with antibiotics is not always the best option and increases the risk of other problems.

At least one-fourth of all the antibiotic prescriptions written in the United States are for ear infections. While Amoxicillin is still considered the first-line drug, penicillin may no longer be effective for many strains of pneumococcus bacteria. Since this is the most common bacterium underlying ear infections, broader spectrum antibiotics are now being used frequently, often for first-line treatment. There appears to be a higher rate of antibiotic-resistant bacterial infections when a child has taken more courses of antibiotics. It is getting harder to treat bacterial infections with antibiotics. There is a now bacteria in the environment no longer susceptible to available antibiotics. As our antibiotics get stronger, so does the bacteria.

Meanwhile children, who have never had an opportunity to fight off an infection because they were always given an antibiotic, have never built up their immune systems. Their body's immune systems have not learned to work effectively because the antibiotics fought off the infection instead.

THE BODY CAN HEAL ITSELF

The osteopathic philosophy states, "The body has an inherent ability to heal itself." This concept is certainly not unique; Hippocrates said it too. Occasionally, the body needs some help. But often, if the body has the right nutrients, exercise, and healthy food and water, it will take care of itself. Even when the body does get sick, it can usually get itself well. We have a wonderful immune system that, when left to do its own fighting, will usually work quite well.

Too often, people view the symptoms of an illness as the illness itself. Fever, cough, and a runny nose are not illnesses. They are the body's efforts to heal. Prescribing antibiotics for an infection may actually interfere with the body's natural abilities. If we allow the antibiotic to do all the work, the immune system may never learn how to fight an infection by itself.

Exposure to bacterial and viral infections allows our immune systems to develop the antibodies that fight off future infections. Antibiotics may interfere with this process, leaving the body vulnerable to future infections. This could be why we are seeing an increase in ear infections at the same time antibiotic use is on the rise.

BACTERIA IS NOT THE UNDERLYING PROBLEM

Fluid in the middle ear that is unable to drain down the Eustachian tube causes recurring ear infections. If the fluid could drain, bacteria would not be able to grow and cause infection. Giving antibiotics to kill the bacteria in the ear is not enough. The antibiotic may kill the bacteria, but it does nothing to help the fluid drain.

There will be times when an antibiotic is necessary and sometimes even life-saving. But overuse and misuse has caused many health problems for our children. If children do need to be on an antibiotic, they should be provided with probiotics during and after the treatment to help prevent the yeast overgrowth.

OTHER CAUSES OF INFLAMMATION IN THE GUT

Parasites or bacteria such as giardia lambdia, crypto-sporidium, blastocystis hominis, helicobacter pylori, klebsiella, citrobacter or pseudomonas found in contaminated food and water can inflame the gut. A routine test for parasites may not be adequate. I use a specialty lab that concentrates on finding these bacteria and parasites and on determining the best treatment, often with dramatic results.

Steroids such as predisone, as well as aspirin, ibuprofen and other non-steroidal anti-inflammatory drugs and prescription hormones like birth control pills can cause gut inflammation. You may think that your child does not take hormones, steroids or even antibiotics. This may not be the case because they are used in the livestock that is raised for food. Even if you think your child has not been prescribed these drugs, significant doses can be ingested from eating conventionally raised meat.

ENZYME DEFICIENCIES

Enzyme deficiencies, like celiac disease and lactose intolerance can also cause problems in the gut. Inability to digest gluten (found in certain grains) and caseine (dairy) may cause its own set of problems.

CELIAC DISEASE

Celiac Disease (CD), which is also known as Celiac Sprue or gluten-sensitivity, is a chronic problem in which gluten products are not digested properly, leaking out into the blood stream causing sensitivity. Patients with full-blown CD often have such symptoms as gastrointestinal distress, diarrhea, fatigue, and failure to grow or gain weight. The toxic effects of the ingested gluten could prove extremely irritating to the nervous system. Some children do better on a gluten-free diet. This diet restricts such foods as wheat, oats, rye, barley and any other grains containing gluten. Some children have an interesting response to caseine and/or gluten when it is not digested properly. Doctors working with children with autism have found that the by-product of improperly digested caseine and/or gluten is Casomorphin and Gliadorphin, respectively. These by-products act like morphine or heroin in the brain and can greatly interfere with the child's ability to function. Parents of many autistic children have reported great improvement in their children by removing all dietary caseine and/or gluten. I have seen the same with some children who had been labeled ADHD. Alternatives to wheat and other gluten products are listed in Figure 15:

Figure 15

Amaranth	Rice Cereal
Brown Rice Flour	Safflower oil
Buckwheat flour groats (Kasha)	Soy (unless intolerant)
Corn meal	Sorgum flour
Lentils	Sugar Cane
Millet	Sweet Potato Flour
Poha	Tapioca Starch
Potato starch	Teff
Potato flour	Yucca
Quinoa Flour	

CASEINE FREE DIET

Caseine, found in dairy products, is one of the most common causes of allergies in children. Because our children are exposed to the protein in cow's milk so young, their bodies become sensitized to it and then suffer from a milk allergy for the rest of their lives. I generally recommend that all my patients avoid cow's milk. Soy and rice milk provide a good alternative to cow's milk.

Step 6—Repair the Gut

Remember:

- The misuse or overuse of antibiotics can cause bacterial resistance and gastrointestinal problems.
- Replacement of good bacteria helps to keep the gut in balance.
- Parasites, bacterial and yeast in the gut are quite common and need to be treated.

STEP 7 — LEARN HOW TO LEARN

It is often assumed that all students by the age of five or six have completed the development of skills needed to be successful in school. However this skill development is not automatic and does not occur magically by a certain age. Some students are unprepared for learning in a structured classroom situation, a problem that can follow them throughout their educational careers. I have seen these children incorrectly labeled as having ADHD, learning disabilities and behavioral problems. Their problem was simply that they were not prepared to learn in a structured classroom setting.

We need to teach children how to learn the way teachers teach. Some children are born knowing how to learn in school. When they walk into the classroom on day one, they understand and do exactly what is expected of them. Their good grades and good citizenship marks reflect this ability. This is how all children should be in school. However, I believe that successful children are actually just natural learners.

There are some people who can sit down at a piano and play by ear even though they have never had a lesson. Well, that would not be true of me. I have never had a piano lesson and I guarantee you, I can't sit down and play by ear. I would need lessons and practice. Just because I don't know how to play the piano, no one is calling me disabled. I'm not going to be placed in a special class for disabled piano players. No one is forcing me to take a drug so that I can focus on the keys and concentrate on the music. I would simply be taught how to play and be given time to practice how to do it. Once I'd learned the basics, I'd be prepared to learn new and more advanced musical scores and be able to keep up with the rest of the piano-playing class. So, we should not be calling children learning disabled or labeling them with ADHD when we haven't prepared them to learn.

HOW WE LEARN

We take in information through our senses. We see, hear, and touch and then process that sensory information. Children in a classroom situation are required to take in information primarily through their eyes and ears. They must be able to listen to the teacher give instructions as well as to see the information on the blackboard and in the textbooks. This is a wonderful system of teaching if that is how a child learns best. But that is probably not the case for your child or you would not be reading this book.

Many children who are experiencing learning difficulties in school are right brain, tactile learners. Right-brain learners are children who tend to use the right or creative side of the brain for learning and processing information. These children tend to be very creative. Tactile or kines-thetic learners learn best with their hands. They like to move around and touch things as they learn. I call these right-brain/tactile-learners, "RBTL's."

Checking your child's vision and hearing will not identify the problem. These children can usually see and hear just fine. When we have our eyesight checked and the doctor says we can see 20/20, that just reflects that we can see clearly at a certain distance. It does not determine how well we process and understand the information we see. Good visual learners, those who find it easy to use their sense of sight to learn, can easily and naturally process and understand the information they see.

The same standard applies to hearing. When you have your hearing checked, that exam only determines how well you can hear sounds. It does not check how well you process and understand the information that you hear. Good auditory learners may find it easier to listen to audiotapes than to read a book. A good visual learner may find it hard to process information through an audiotape or through verbal instructions and may prefer to see the information written instead. Although "RBTL" children may see and hear perfectly well, the brain of the "RBTL" child does not process the information through the eyes and ears as easily. They prefer to learn through touch instead.

"RBTL" children can be frustrated because schools are set up to accommodate left-brain, logical, auditory and visual learners who are perfectly adept at looking at the blackboard and listening to the teacher lecture. When the educational system assumes that every child is using the left side of the brain and is an auditory and visual learner, it makes standardized education very difficult on the "RBTL" student.

IDENTIFYING THE PROBLEM

In the early school years, because "RBTL" children are often very smart, they compensate. But by the fourth or fifth grade, the teaching system becomes more structured. The teacher stands in front of the class, lecturing and writing assignments on the black board while the children are expected to take notes and write assignments down correctly. Although "RBTL" children see and hear the information, their brains don't process it through the auditory and visual senses very well. They are still going to try to learn, but because they are tactile learners, they may pick up their pencil and flip it, put their hands in their pockets or on the person in front of them and promptly get in trouble when all they were trying to do was learn the best way they know how.

Although they are very bright, these children often get labeled as learning disabled or ADHD. Sometimes they are placed in special classes where they are taught with a smaller group, can get special attention, and are perhaps even allowed to learn through their tactile sense.

HELPING THE TACTILE LEARNER

In my office children often play in the same room while I sit and talk to their parents. I have toys in the room and usually the children are over in the corner playing. These are creative children so it is quite common to see them playing creatively, making up stories and talking out loud with great expression. Anyone watching a child playing in this way would think that they were totally engrossed and oblivious to everything else, but that is not the case. These children listen. A parent will tell me something, and out of nowhere, the child will contribute to the consultation. These children hear every single word that we've said because they are being allowed to listen the way they listen best, while moving around and playing. Unfortunately, for these children this is not acceptable classroom behavior.

LET'S GET PHYSICAL

Physical activity is very important. None of us can sit still and concentrate for long periods of time. We need to take a break, get up and stretch, move our bodies and get our circulation going. This physical break is even more important for children who have an even shorter attention span than adults. They have a greater physiological need to be active. When a child is fidgety and having difficulty concentrating, it is time for a break. I recommend that parents allow their children to stop studying every 30-minutes and take a five minute break. Parents have reported this actually cut overall study time. Most children concentrate better after a break.

The physical activity of recess revives energy and alertness so that the child returns to class more attentive and ready to learn. Physical play is an active form of learning essential to development and the promotion of the gross motor skills necessary for learning. It enhances perceptual abilities through interaction and movement in a three-dimensional environment. Play reduces tension and helps the child relax. If the child has adrenaline on board as a result of an allergic reaction or from too much sugar and not enough protein, the activity will help expend it, bringing the body back to a calm, more chemically balanced state. Some parents have told me that their child has been denied recess at school as a punishment for bad behavior in class. This is the opposite of what should occur. A child who is having difficulty sitting needs more time to move around, not less.

The following is quick guide to help identify if a child is an RBTL. If your answer is "Yes" to several of the following questions, it is a good possibility that the child is RBTL and could benefit from programs designed to develop auditory and visual skills.

Figure 16
RBTL Guide

1. My child has difficulty remembering left from right.
2. My child does not understand how the directions of North and South on a map relate to the world.
3. My child is not very coordinated or good at sports.
4. My child has difficulty throwing a ball into an intended receptacle, such as basketball into the goal or a paper wad into the garbage can.
5. My child has trouble jumping rope.
6. My child does not seem to hear me when I call but his/her hearing is fine.
7. My child seems to wiggle and move all the time and when asked is unable to sit still.
8. My child touches everything of interest.
9. My child seems to get confused when asked to follow simple directions.
10. My child has trouble with handwriting.
11. My child is forgetful, unorganized and sometimes confused over what is expected of him/her.
12. My child has difficulty remembering more than one verbal request at a time.
13. My child describes things using "tactile" words such as "That doesn't feel good" and "You hurt my feelings"
14. My child is sensitive about how things feel-complains that clothing is too scratchy, or stiff and hurts.
15. My child has difficulty understanding cause and effect-does not seem to understand simple consequences to specific actions.

UNDERSTANDING VOCABULARY

Sometimes, a child's learning problem is due to not understanding the actual words used in instruction. In mathematics many words have the same meaning. Instead of "subtract" a teacher might use "less," "take away" or "minus." If a teacher is inconsistent or has not clarified definitions, a young child might be very confused and have no idea what the word means in the context in which it is being used. It can be helpful to give a child an age-appropriate dictionary for home and school. Playing word definition games with the child while driving or while shopping can help expand the vocabulary. Exploring words can help establish a habit of curiosity about language and the confidence to ask the meaning of unknown words.

WHAT TO DO

Many programs are available to help children develop visual and auditory learning skills. "Vision Therapy" is available through developmental optometrists and auditory processing programs enhance the ability to listen. Sensory Integration works to strengthen the sensory skills. Occupational therapists and physical therapists work with children with learning differences. I have developed a home program from which I took what I believe to be the best of the established developmental activities. [*See Resource section.*]

OTHER HELPFUL TOOLS

Tactile learners need something to fiddle with while they learn. It not only keeps them quiet in the classroom but it also enhances their learning. I first recommended a small stress ball because they are quiet and "feel" good. But unfortunately the balls ended up being thrown around the room and disrupting the class. Now I suggest using a smooth stone with a chain through it, like a key chain. The chain can be attached to a belt loop or a buttonhole so the child doesn't lose it and always has it on hand to help them in class. The same object or a similar one can also be used during homework time.

THE MOZART EFFECT

Don Campbell's book, *The Mozart Effect*, explains how listening to Mozart's music can help focus and concentration. I agree and recommend these children use headphones that also block outside distractions. Parents report excellent results, indicating that the combined use of headphones and an object with which to fiddle cut their child's homework time in half. I will often write a prescription for the child to be allowed to use the headphones in school. If the teacher has given them instructions to sit quietly and work, then they can put on the headphones, listen to the Mozart and often get their work completed more quickly and more accurately.

GIFTED CHILDREN

Some people have compared ADHD and gifted behaviors and found them to be very similar. This does not surprise me because so many of the children I see in my office who have been labeled ADHD, are actually gifted. They are very, very bright. Here is a comparison of the behaviors for you to judge.

You can see a lot of similarities in the comparison list. It is time to recognize that these children are not really

Figure 17	
ADHD Behaviors	**Gifted Behaviors**
Poor sustained attention	Poor attention, boredom and daydreaming
Lack of persistence on task	Low tolerance for persistence with tasks that appear irrelevant
Impulsivity	Judgment often lags behind their intellect
Difficulty regulating behavior in social settings	Power struggles over behavior
Active and restless	High activity level and needs less sleep
Difficulty adhering to rules and regulations	Questions rules and regulations

ADHD but are gifted. I believe we are chemically destroying our best and brightest children by drugging them and altering their personalities and their potential. Albert Einstein had a lot of problems in school. He didn't talk until he was six years old and actually failed math. He eventually dropped out of school because he couldn't learn the way he was being taught. I am sure that today, if he were alive, he would be labeled ADHD and be prescribed Ritalin®.

Step 7—Learn How to Learn

Remember:

- All children do not learn in the same way.
- Tactile learners will have more difficulties in school.
- Children can be taught to be better auditory and visual learners.
- Tactile learners need something to fiddle with while they learn.
- Listening to Mozart's music may help concentration.
- A child who has been labeled ADHD may instead be gifted.

STEP 8 — CLEAR THE HEAD WITH OMT

OMT MEANS OSTEOPATHIC MANIPULATIVE TREATMENT

As an osteopathic physician, a DO (Doctor of Osteopathic Medicine), we learn healing can be accomplished by using something other than drugs and surgery. It is osteopathic manipulation treatment(OMT). In addition to what is taught in MD schools, the Osteopathic schools also teach approximately 150 course hours on the musculo-skeletal system and the use of OMT. This century-old treatment has been used effectively for more than just structural problems, such as a "bad back." OMT has saved lives. Before there were antibiotics, many people died of flu and other infections. Osteopathic physicians used OMT to help boost the patient's immune system and to aid the body in fighting off the infection. During the deadly Swine Flu epidemic in the early 1900's, the death rate for patients of osteopathic physicians who used OMT was much lower than those of MDs.

The first time I learned about the benefits of OMT was many years ago when my young daughter was experiencing a severe allergic reaction to mosquito bites. Her legs would become very swollen and she would actually need crutches to help her walk because of the pain. This happened almost every time she was bitten and it would take days for the swelling and pain to resolve. During one of these episodes, I took her to an osteopathic physician who said she needed OMT to help reduce the swelling and to assist the body in removing the toxins from her system. He explained that it was a gentle procedure so I decided to try it. He was very gentle and so was the treatment and it was remarkably effective. The swelling began to reduce almost immediately and within hours of the treatment was gone. During medical school, I worked hard at learning OMT. I knew I wanted to use it in my practice and I have, with excellent results.

THE OSTEOPATHIC PHILOSOPHY

In medical school, we also learned about the Osteopathic Philosophy, "the body has an inherent ability to heal itself." Sometimes the body needs assistance to do its job. That's when, as an osteopathic physician, I help remove barriers to healing and support the body in its work. Although I do prescribe drugs when needed, I don't just prescribe them to cover symptoms except in acute cases and for short periods of time. My goal is to help each patient find and treat the underlying cause of their symptoms. Simply treating symptoms does not solve the problem in the long run. There is too great a likelihood that the problem will return. By just treating the symptoms we end up with chronic health problems that never seem to go away.

GENTLE OMT TECHNIQUES

Leaning both OMT and the Osteopathic Philosophy has helped me to see illness differently. In addition to looking for the underlying causes of illnesses, I learned to use my hands to help the body to work better and to heal. I use only the gentle techniques that involve working with soft tissues such as connective tissues and the muscles. Osteopathic physicians can use their hands to help the body's nervous, vascular and immune systems to better function. This wonderful approach has many applications today.

OMT FOR ATTENTION
AND BEHAVIOR SYMPTOMS

I find that most of the children who are diagnosed with ADHD also have had chronic ear and respiratory infections. These chronic infections affect how a child feels and acts and can definitely affect learning ability. This is particularly true of children who have chronic ear infections. The fluid in the ears can impair hearing, which can delay development and limit learning. Children with allergies suffer from congestion even when they do not have an infection. Either way, the child is simply not at his or her best a great deal of the time. No one does their best work when they don't feel well.

DR. BLOCK'S OMT
TREATMENT FOR CHILDREN

I developed an OMT treatment to help boost the immune system and to drain the head and neck of fluid. It doesn't matter if the fluid is from allergies or an infection. The technique, much like a massage, is relaxing, feels good, and most children like it. I tested the treatment on a group of patients who had suffered with chronic ear infections for months and some even for years. The results were excellent. I compared the amount of fluid in the ears before and immediately after my treatment with a tympanogram, an objective test that determines if there is fluid in the ear. All of the children had a significant amount of fluid. After a five-minute OMT treatment, I re-tested each child and the tympanogram showed significant improvement of the fluid level. More treatments continued to reduce and to prevent the fluid. One hundred percent of the patients got well. Most resolved within three weeks. Some of the children in my study were scheduled for surgery to place tubes in their ears to relieve the fluid. Needless to say, these children were spared an unnecessary and invasive medical procedure. In a study that appeared in the April 19, 2001, issue of *The New England Journal of Medicine*, researchers found that placing tubes in the children's ears did not measurably improve speech, psychological, or developmental outcomes.

PARENTS LEARN OMT

Although I continue to use my OMT treatment in my office for my patients, the effectiveness of the treatment led me to begin teaching parents how to do the treatment at home. I expected the treatment would help with infections and fluid but in the hands of parents, we found even more benefits. Parents came back to me and said, "You know, when I use that treatment on my child they are not as foggy. They are more clear-headed and they can think better." So I started recommending that parents use the treatment right before their child goes to school in the morning. Since there is a documented correlation between allergies and learning problems, OMT, practiced at home, could be of great benefit for a child whose learning problems are caused, in some part, by their allergies. A child suffering with allergies has a lot of mucus in their sinuses. Just like a person with a head cold this leaves the child feeling groggy, irritable, agitated and unable to think clearly. My OMT treatment is very simple and takes less then five minutes. It can help relieve many symptoms to help a child feel better. A child who feels better can learn better.

OTHER USES FOR OMT

I use my OMT treatment for any respiratory infection including the flu and the common cold. It can be used on adults as well. I know one patient, who lives alone, who performed the treatment on herself when she had the flu. It not only made her feel better at the time by relieving the pressure, but she felt that it also helped her get better sooner.

HOW TO DO OMT AT HOME

The OMT procedure is explained below. I have also produced a video, *Treat Ear and Respiratory Infections WITHOUT Antibiotics,* for those who want to learn the OMT treatment and find it easier to watch a demonstration. (*See Resource Section.*)

OSTEOPATHIC MANIPULATION (OMT) FOR EAR AND RESPIRATORY INFECTIONS

I recommend that my patients perform the OMT treatment three (3) times each day when the child has allergy symptoms or an infection. Using this treatment encourages the fluids to drain properly and to help the lymph system, which is responsible for removing toxins from the body, function more effectively.

Some parents use OMT through the night if the child wakes up with discomfort. They report that it helps the child go back to sleep. In general, I think it is helpful to continue using the treatment a minimum of one time per day to prevent fluid build up. It can also help to boost the immune system.

Step 1

1.

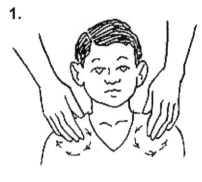

With the child on her/ his back and the parent at the child's head, the parent's fingers are placed half way between the end of the child's shoulder and neck on each side of the upper chest. Then the fingers are placed just below the collarbone. That's the bone that runs across each side of the chest just below the shoulder. There might be a slight indentation under the fingers, just below the collarbone. This area can be tender when pressed. It may feel like a small, round pebble-like structure at that point. This area is then gently massaged in a circular motion for approximately 30-45 seconds.

Step 2

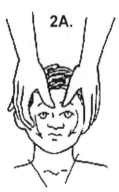

2A.

A. Thumbs are placed firmly on the middle of child's forehead. Using gentle pressure, rub the thumbs from the center of the forehead outward to the hairline and then down the side of the cheeks. This is repeated three to four times.

B. Next with the same type of pressure, starting under the eye-socket on top of the sinuses the thumbs are run down the sides of the nose and across the cheeks, along the cheek bone.

C. Then the thumbs are run down one side of the face, starting at the temple, moving down the cheek, under the chin and down the neck. One side of the neck is done at a time. This is done on the back of the neck as well. The fluids in the head are always pushed downward toward the heart.

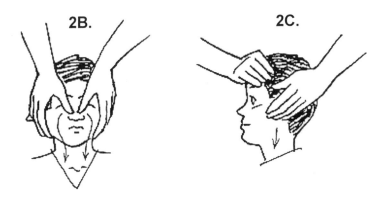

Step 3
With the child still lying on his or her back, the flat part of the hand is gently but firmly pushed up against the child's rib cage several times, stretching the muscles that lie between the ribs. This is repeated on the other side.

Step 4

A. The child's leg is held at the foot with one hand and the other hand is cupped around the ankle. With a firm, gentle, motion, the hand slides up the leg to just above the knee. This is one long smooth stroke. The hand is not lifted until the top of the leg is reached. This is repeated on the other leg.

B. This same movement is done on the child's arms. One arm is held at the hand and the other hand is around the wrist. With a firm, gentle, motion, the hand slides up the arm. This is one long smooth stroke. The hand is not lifted until the top of the arm is reached. This is repeated on the other arm.

If this treatment is helpful in clearing the fluids from a child's head, it may allow that child to concentrate and behave better in school.

4A.

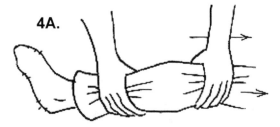

4B.

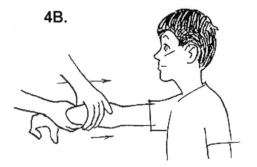

Step 8—Clear the Head With OMT

Remember:

- Children with allergies may have fluid in their sinuses, which interferes with learning.
- Draining the fluid with gentle osteopathic massage may allow the child to concentrate and behave better.

STEP 9 — STAND UP FOR YOUR CHILD

No one but you is going to stand up for your child. My mother taught me that you do whatever is necessary to help your child. I learned that lesson well. That is why I went to medical school to save my daughter. I had to do whatever was necessary to get her well again. If you are reading this book, you are probably that kind of parent too. Let me share with you some of the ways in which parents can stand up for their children.

1. KNOW THE LAW AND YOUR RIGHTS AS A PARENT.

Know the laws in your state and make sure no one is infringing on them. It is necessary in order to protect your children. Contact your State's Department of Education or Board of Education. Ask for a copy of the laws and regulations that govern the state's teachers. It is a federal law that school personnel cannot push you or even encourage you to drug your child. If you know and understand your rights, the school cannot take advantage of you or your child.

2. BE YOUR CHILD'S ADVOCATE.

Many parents tell me that at the start of a school year they plan to tell the new teacher how difficult the last year was for their child in order to prepare the new teacher in hopes of working together toward a better year. I tell them <u>NO</u>! Don't prepare the teacher to expect a problem with your child! I have seen students blossom and excel with another teacher simply because the child is perceived differently by the new instructor. I cited a good example earlier in mentioning the child who took a vitamin instead of a drug to pacify a teacher who had recommended the boy be tested for ADHD. The child had never had any problems in school prior to that year. The teacher said she had seen great improvement with children on Ritalin®. The mother gave her child vitamins but told the teacher he was taking a morning dose of his "treatment" which the teacher assumed was Ritalin®. In no time, in the teacher's eyes, the boy had improved. She saw what she wanted to see.

The ADHD label is completely subjective. A negative opinion a teacher forms may be more about perception than fact. Tell teachers all the good things about your children. Let the teacher find out if there are any problems. And if problems do exist, hopefully they will be balanced with all the positive things you've brought to the teacher's attention.

3. HELP YOUR CHILD MAKE A GOOD FIRST IMPRESSION

Identify what it is that your child does best and let the teacher know. Keep the teacher focused on the good things. Consider that your child might be gifted and look at their behaviors and abilities from that perspective. I always considered the first day of school to be very important for my child. When my own children were young, I started planning for that first day during the summer. I would find out which children would be in their classes and invite one or two over to play. This allowed my children to feel comfortable and to have a friend in class that first day at school. I wanted them to feel confident. I always made sure that they had all the supplies they needed and were well dressed and squeaky clean.

Next I would find something special about them to magnify for the teacher's benefit. For instance, my son could tell time on an analog clock before he even began kindergarten. Most children can read a digital watch or clock but reading an analog, at age 5, was exceptional. I bought him a large analog watch to wear to school. I wanted the teacher to know that he had these abilities, so she would assess him by his best qualities not his weaknesses. Every year on the first day of school, I took their picture before we left the house. I considered it a special day and wanted them to feel excited and positive about it. Doing this each year, I think, helped set the stage for a successful year.

4. DO NOT LET YOUR CHILD SUFFER UNNECESSARY CONSEQUENCES

It is often said that we should let our children learn from the consequences of their actions. I think this is cruel. Children learn best through positive experiences, not negative ones. Sometimes our children simply make a mistake. After all, no one is perfect. When we make a mistake, we don't just lie down and take the consequences. We try to fix the problem. We need to teach our children how to fix the problem as well as how to prevent it in the future. For instance, I do not think it is helpful for a child to get an "F" on a paper just because he or she forgot to bring home a book or assignment. Doing so hurts their self-esteem and it reduces their image to the teacher. My philosophy is to teach the child skills to help them remember the assignment for the next time, but also to help them get the assignment for the immediate crisis first. Let them call a friend to borrow the book or go back to school and get whatever is needed. Just help them succeed. Be their advocate and coach.

That's what my mother was for me. When I was in school, we were required to write long theme papers. I did not know how to do it. No one taught me how to write these papers, they were just assigned. I was concerned and totally unprepared. My mother helped me write my papers. At the same time, she helped me learn how to do it. Later, I was able to write them on my own. It didn't hurt me to have my mother help me in this way, certainly not in the long run. Today I am a doctor and an author. You are reading my fourth book. My first book, *No More Ritalin®* is a top-seller and my second, *No More Antibiotics,* won a national award. I learned to write, but the most important thing I learned was that I could count on my mother to help me succeed in school and to preserve my self-esteem at the same time.

5. PROVIDE POSITIVE FEEDBACK TO YOUR CHILD

We all know how important it is to focus on the positive but it can make a remarkable change for the better when used to help children learn. I recommend that we see only the best in our children. It can be very damaging to compare one child to another. Everyone has strengths in some area. Children, who struggle in reading, may be very creative and excel in art. Acknowledge the child's ability and provide them with opportunities to do well. Sign up for an art class. Keep art materials at home. Frame your child's pictures and put them on the wall. You can also provide opportunities for your child to help someone else learn to draw. This makes a very strong statement to your child that they have valuable abilities. It builds self-esteem. It also teaches your child that it is okay not to know how to do everything and that people can help each other learn. All children want to learn and want to please us. We just have to help them by making sure they have all the tools and support they need.

6. DO NOT LET THE SCHOOL TEST YOUR CHILD FOR ADHD

I always recommend that parents not allow the school to do psychological testing on their children. If a child is having problems in school, a test will not only serve to provide a label for the child but will also become part of their official records. The results of the testing can follow students throughout their educational career. The most common diagnosis to come out of this kind of testing is, of course, ADHD. It is subjective and will provide no real benefit for the child's problem. The diagnosis allows the physician to drug the child and the school to document another ADHD student. Don't forget that public schools receive money for every child who has the ADHD label. I do not want to see another child become just another dollar sign. The best way to protect a child is to not let the school test him or her psychologically.

7. BREAK THE SILENCE

Some parents have found that one of the most powerful ways to stand up for a child is to go public when the schools or the doctors try to harm them. Parents have said that it helps to talk to just one person or to the world. I believe that exposing the schools and the doctors and holding them accountable for their actions not only warns other parents of the problem but also can help each child. First, it tells the child that they are okay and that the parent does not believe the school or the doctor is correct. Speaking out also helps to identify other parents in the same position with whom one can share information and provide support.

One of the best examples of "Going Public" is the story of Patty Weathers and her son Michael who were mentioned in Step 2. As you recall, Patty was pressured by the New York schools to put her child on drugs. He had already been on several psychiatric drugs and had suffered side effects from each. So, Patty took him off the drugs but the school insisted he be medicated again. That's when Patty decided to bring Michael to Texas to see me. The school had already turned her into Child Protective Services for neglect. When I first saw Michael, I learned that he had not had a complete check-up before or during his drug treatment. I see this in my practice everyday, hundreds of children placed on dangerous and potent drugs without so much as a blood test, much less an EKG to assure that the heart is okay before prescribing a psychiatric drug with possible cardiac consequences. This is such a common form of medical negligence, it should make us all angry.

During my work-up on Michael, I found that he was anemic, had nutritional deficiencies and allergies, any of which can cause learning and behavior difficulties. When these conditions were treated Michael's symptoms abated. The Weathers took Michael out of public school and enrolled him in private school, continuing my protocol. Months later Michael continues to do very well.

Relieved that her child was okay and drug-free, Patty had time to reflect on her experience. Knowing the injustice of the school's position and the close call her child had from the pressure to inappropriately drug him, Patty began to speak out. Not just to her friends and community — Patty went national. She was on national shows airing on NBC, ABC and CBS and her story appeared in newspapers across the country. We were both guests on *The Montel Williams Show* and Patty even testified at Federal Legislative Hearings.

Perhaps it was Patty's voice that helped another New York family who was also pressured to put their child on drugs. When they refused, the school turned the parents in to Child Protective Services for neglect. This time, the parents ended up in the New York courts. There the judge ruled that the parents were required to give their child Ritalin®. It was court-ordered drugging of a child. The news picked up both stories and the press followed the court case, reporting every detail. After a great deal of publicity, it was later decided that it was not necessary to drug this child. Forcing our schools, medical system and courts to work in the open can not only be a cause for change, but can also encourage people to act more responsibly in the first place.

8. CHANGE SCHOOLS IF YOUR CHILD'S SAFETY DEPENDS ON IT.

Patty was fortunate to be able to put Michael in a private school that meets his emotional and academic needs. But sometimes such a school is not available or is too expensive for the family. There are other options. I have seen families request another public school or if needed, actually move to another school district for their child's benefit. And there is one other option that has gained growing acceptance and popularity. It's *Home Schooling!* Today, home schooling is so widespread that there is an educational industry providing excellent curriculum support for the teaching parent. There is also a whole network of families working together, preventing social isolation for the children. Home-schooled children seem to not only learn faster in a shorter amount of time, but to get more time for physical and social activities. A recent report stated that a group of home-schooled students who just turned college age excelled at the entrance test and in their course work. If the school is an oppressive, negative experience for a child, if they want to label and drug the child, other school situations might be considered.

Step 9—Stand Up For Your Child

Remember:

- Parents should stand up for their children.
- Know state and federal laws and rights.
- Be an advocate.
- Make a good first impression.
- No unnecessary consequences.
- Positive feedback.

STEP 10 — CONSIDER OTHER UNDERLYING CAUSES

I've already explained most of the common causes I find which include allergies, hypoglycemia, too much sugar, diet problems, nutritional deficiencies and digestive and learning problems which cause the ADHD symptoms. I also find other causes worth mentioning.

1. HEAVY METAL TOXICITY

Aside from the often-publicized lead poisoning problem, there are other heavy metal problems of which many doctors seem to be unaware and which could be overlooked. Some children show a build up of mercury in their bodies. This can be caused by mercury injected into the child's body through vaccinations. Mercury is used as a preservative in vaccines. By the time children have finished their first round of vaccinations, they may have received a level of mercury that exceeds what the Environmental Protection Agency (EPA) recognizes as a safe level. Mercury toxicity can cause learning and behavioral problems. There are tests that can identify this heavy metal in the body and treatments to help remove it but they are not standard or run routinely by most conventional doctors.

2.THYROID PROBLEMS

A thyroid profile is a simple test to run. If a problem shows up it can be easily treated. Yet most children I see have never had their thyroid checked. Here are some of the symptoms for thyroid problems.

Hyperthyroidism (overactive thyroid)
Restlessness, nervousness, irritability, erratic behavior, overactivity

Insomnia

Headaches

Weight loss with increased appetite

Decreased attention span, "brain fog"

Heart palpitations, increased heart rate, and breathlessness

Heat intolerance, increased sweating, warm moist skin, tremors, shakiness, trembling, jitteriness, trembling hands

Vision and eye problems, protrusion of eyes, staring gaze

Increased frequency of stools, diarrhea

Fine skin

Hypothyroidism (low functioning thyroid)
Fatigue, easily tired, difficulty waking up in the morning, low energy

Poor memory, headaches, forgetfulness, memory loss

Gradual personality change, irritability, depression

Cold intolerance, cold hands and feet, low body temperature

Dry sparse hair, dry skin, rough pale skin

Weight gain despite loss of appetite, constipation, problems digesting fats and oils,

Puffiness around the eyes, facial and hand puffiness

Swelling in front of neck, trouble swallowing
Slow pulse, low blood pressure
Slow speech, hoarse voice
Dull facial expression
Sore muscles, painful joints

Hyperthyroid or Hypothyroid can interfere with learning and behavior, so if a child has several of these symptoms, a thyroid test should be performed.

4. INCONSISTENT PARENTING

It is extremely important for children to know what is expected of them and to have consistency from both parents. Even if the parents are not together, the children need to see that the parents are going to agree on the parenting decisions. I believe that if parents are having difficulty agreeing, it is better to defer to the parent who spends the most time with the child. Parenting classes can be found, but be sure that the person teaching the class has similar values to your own.

These are just a few of the other possible factors that may cause ADHD symptoms. Although I find that the ones I've explained in this book are the most common, your child is unique. No one knows him or her better than you. So it is important for you to see this final step as not the end of the process, but the beginning of a lifetime of looking for ways to help your child. That's what parenting is all about. We spend time finding the best for our children as they grow up, from the best school, summer camp, music class, neighborhood, college and more. We never stop helping our children. Once we have children we are always parents. Our children need us especially when they are young and are having problems. That's when we must

Step 10—Consider Other Underlying Causes

go the extra mile. One of the most important things that can be done for them when answers do not come easily is to continue the search and to stay open. Do not dismiss possible answers for the child's problem just because they are new ideas or because a doctor or school discounts them. I didn't give up on my daughter even though it was an uphill battle all the way. I believe that she is healthy today because I never quit looking and trying new treatments. So, keep searching and stay open to the answers. I know it can be a long and difficult road but it so worth the effort. Nothing is more precious or more important than our children.

Step 10—Consider Other Underlying Causes

Remember:

- Keep an open mind.
- Never stop looking for solutions.
- Be consistent with parenting.

If more parents pursued these steps
to improve their children's attention and
behavior there could be a time

When there would be No More Schools
pushing drugs for "ADHD"
When there would be No More Doctors
prescribing drugs for "ADHD"
When there would be No More children
taking drugs for "ADHD"

Because there would be

No More ADHD.

CONCLUSION

Attention Deficit Hyperactivity Disorder, (ADHD) is a negative, psychiatric label that psychiatrists voted into existence by a show of hands at an annual meeting. ADHD could just as well stand for **A**nother **D**octor **H**anding-out **D**rugs. I do not believe that ADHD has anything to do with our children. In my opinion, and in my experience, ADHD does not exist. There are many health and learning problems that can cause attention and behavior symptoms in children. I find and fix them everyday in my office. My 10-Step program addresses the problems I most often find that affect my young patients. I believe these *10 Steps to Help Improve Attention and Behavior WITHOUT Drugs* can help to pave the road, one step at a time, to a brighter future for our children and to No More ADHD.

THE 10-STEPS

Step 1: Understand the Medical System
Step 2: Educate Yourself on the School System
Step 3: Dump the Sugar
Step 4: Take Your A, B, C's, Vitamins, That Is
Step 5: Attack the Allergies
Step 6: Repair the Gut
Step 7: Learn How to Learn
Step 8: Clear the Head with OMT
Step 9: Stand Up for Your Child
Step 10: Consider Other Underlying Causes

RESOURCES

The Block Center

1750 Norwood Drive
Hurst, Texas 76054
(817) 280-9933
(888) DrBlock (372-5625)
www.blockcenter.com

OTHER HEALTH AND EDUCATIONAL PROGRAMS/PRODUCTS FROM DR. MARY ANN BLOCK

The Road To No More Ritalin® Seminar with Dr. Mary Ann Block-Video

In this seminar, Dr. Block not only exposes the dangers of drugs and the limits of our current medical system but she also offers practical and helpful information for parents. Dr. Block explains the 10 Steps to Help Improve Your Child's Attention and Behavior WITHOUT Drugs.

The Learn-How-To-Learn Program® A Program to Help Develop Learning Skills- Workbook and Video

This interactive program was developed by Dr. Mary Ann Block to help students of all ages learn. The Learn-How-To-Learn Program provides activities to help develop the necessary skills for learning.

Resources

Read-With-Ease® Highlighter Bookmarks™

Instantly helps to improve comfort, clarity and comprehension. Lay a colored Read-with-Ease® Bookmark flat on the page and read through it. The Bookmarks can mark your page, help track your reading place, increase your reading pace and reduce eye fatigue. Most people can see better and more clearly with less stress to read more comfortably, longer.

Treat Ear and Respiratory Infections WITHOUT Antibiotics! Using Osteopathic Principles, Practices, and Gentle Massage At Home! — Video

In this video Dr. Block demonstrates gentle techniques based on a century-old philosophy of osteopathic medicine which she taught in medical school. This technique helps to drain ears and upper respiratory tract and boost the immune system without antibiotics. Dr. Block explains, in easy-to-understand terms, what you can do at home to treat and help prevent future infections.

Learning with Mozart Audiotape, Music to Help Students Focus

Music has been shown to have a positive effect on people. Some research has shown that people who listen to music by Mozart can feel more relaxed, heal faster, and may even learn easier. It appears that the optimum effect of music may occur while actually listening to it. That is why Dr. Block recommends listening to music by Mozart while reading, studying, and doing other learning activities. To help the students focus and concentrate better , Dr. Block recommends that her patients listen to Mozart using ear phones to block out outside noises to reduce distractions. Many parents have reported that homework time is cut in half. Parents like using the tape for their reading and work as well.

Back-To-School Tools: A Learning Seminar with Dr. Mary Ann Block-Audio Tape

In this one-hour seminar, Dr. Block discusses the basic three factors that need to be in place for learning to occur and how parents can provide them. Dr. Block explains some of the hidden health issues that cause barriers to learning. She clarifies why some children do not learn well in a structured classroom setting and how parents can help prepare their child for school. Dr. Block explains some quick tools that can enhance learning styles and she lists her "Top Ten Learning Tips."

NUTRITION For-Your-Kids™ Vitamin and Mineral Drink , contains twenty nutrients and no sugar. And it taste great!

This good-tasting mix was developed by Dr. Mary Ann Block as a supplement for children who have difficulty swallowing tablets. Many of these children also have food sensitivities. That is why Dr. Block formulated Nutrition For-Your-Kids™ without yeast, wheat, corn, dairy or sugar. These nutrients are free of most common plant and animal allergens, (antigens) and do not contain preservatives, dilutents, or chemical additives. Mix with 8 oz. of soy milk, milk or other preferred drink. May also be sprinkled on cereal.

CONCENTRATION For-Your-Kids™ is designed to

support your child's ability to concentrate. DMAE, a substance normally found in the brain, helps promote mental concentration.* Concentration For-Your-Kids™ contains: Magnesium, Zinc, L-Aspartate, DMAE, Standardized Soybean Lecithin (LECI-PS®), and Grape Seed Extract. Kids like its sweet tart flavor.

DHA For-Your-Kids™ is a fatty acid that the brain

uses for its growth and function. DHA is naturally found in fresh fish and other foods that your child may not enjoy. Many active children have been found to have a special dietary need for essential fatty acids, including DHA.* Contains: Docosahexaenoic Acid (DHA) (from algal oil [Neuromins®])

* These statements have not been evaluated by the Food and Drug Administration. This Product is not intended to diagnose, treat, cure or prevent any disease. Consult your doctor before making changes to any existing healthcare program

The Food-4-Kids© Program was developed by Dr. Block and is a helpful method for organizing, planning and preparing meals on a rotation diet. It is flexible enough to allow personalizations based on food preferences, cookbook diet plans, specific recipes and healthcare provider recommendations. The kit contains instructions and a magnetic board with more than 150 food magnets to help parents set up and change meals for a four-day food cycle. Written instructions and a video by Dr. Block explains the Food-4-Kids© program.

ORGANIZATIONS

College of Optometry of Visual Development
"Evaluates eyes and vision to assess how the visual system affects human development, individual performance and quality of life."
covd.org   1-888.covd770

DFW area: Ken Lane, OD
230 Main Street, Lewisville, TX 75057
klane@123go.com   972-221-2564

Resources

Lindamood-Bell
"Learning Enhancement"
lindamoodbell.com   800-233-1819

DFW area: 5600 Lover's Lane, suite 230, Dallas 75204
214-358-0688,   800-300-1818

Sensory Integration (SI)
"SI is the function of the brain that is responsible for producing a composite picture of who we are, where we are
and what is going on around us."
sensoryint.com   310-320-2335

DFW area:
SI Challenge
"Senses Working Together to Achieve Balance"
SI-Challenge.org   214-528-6423

Fast ForWord
"Using brain research and technology to enhance human
learning and performance
FastForWord.com   888-665-7707

Tomatis
"Builds strong listening skills through auditory stimulation to improve learning and language abilities, communication, creativity and social behavior"
tomatis.com

DFW area: The Listening Center
tomatis@dallas.net   972-404-8152

National Association for Child Development (NACD)
"Helps children and adults reach their full potential"
nacd.org   801-621-8606

Resources

DFW area:
dallas@nacd.org   817-460-3323

Celiac Sprue Association/USA
402-558-0600 (Omaha, Nebraska)
Canadian Celiac Association
905-567-7195 (Toronto)

Gluten Intolerance Group of North America
P.O. Box 23053
Seattle, Washington
407-856-3754

Celiac Disease Foundation
13251 Ventura Blvd. Suite #3
Studio City, CA 91604
818-990-2354

Citizen's Commission for Human Rights (CCHR)
"Founded to investigate and expose psychiatric violations
of human rights"
800-869-2247

The National Vaccine Information Center (NVIC)
"To prevent vaccine injuries and deaths through public
education"
909shot.com   800-909-shot

The Autism Research Institute
"A World Center for Research and Information on Autism
and Other Severe Behavioral Handicaps in Children"
autism.com/ari   619-281-7165

Defeat Autism Now (DAN) information
autism.com/ari/dan

Resources

Feingold Association
P.O. Box 6550
Alexandria, VA 22306
(703) 768-FAUS

BIBLIOGRAPHY

Attention Deficit Disorder: A Dubious Diagnosis. The Merrow Report. Public Broadcasting. October 29, 1995.

Barkley, A., Russell, M. Fischer, et al. "The Adolescent Outcome of Hyperactive Children Diagnosed by Research Criteria: An 8-Year Prospective Follow-Up Study." *Journal of the American Academy of Child and Adolescent Psychiatry* 29 no. 4 (July 1990): 546-556.

Barkley, R. A., M. B. McMurray, C. S. Edelbrook, K. Robbins. "Side Effects of Methylphenidate in Children with Attention Deficit Disorder: A Systematic, Placebo-Controlled Evaluation." *Pediatrics* 86 (1990): 184-192.

Bhagavan, H. N., M. Coleman, D. B. Coursin. "The Effect of Pyridoxine Hydrochloride on Blood Serotonin and Pyridoxal Phosphate Contents in Hyperactive Children." *Pediatrics* 55 no. 3. (March 1975): 437-441.

Block, M. A., *No More Ritalin®: Treating ADHD Without Drugs.* New York: Kensington Books, 1996.

_____. *No More Antibiotics: Treating Ear and Respiratory Infections Naturally.* New York: Kensington Books, 1998

Bock, S., Hugh Sampson, et al. "Double-Blind Placebo Controlled Food Challenge (DBPCFC) as an Office Procedure: A Manual." *Journal of Allergy Clinical Immunology* 82 (December 1988): 986-997.

"Change Special Education." *Fort Worth Star-Telegram* 29 July 1999.

Ciba-Geigy, Ritalin® Brochure, 1995

Bibliography

Coleman, et al. "A Preliminary Study of the Effect of Pyridoxine
Administration to a Subgroup of Hyperkinetic Children: A Double-Blind, Crossover Comparison with
Methylphenidate." *Biological Psychiatry* 14 no. 5
(1979): 741-751.

Coleman, N., et al. "DMAE in the Treatment of Hyperactive
Children." *Psychosomatics* 17 (1976): 68-72.

Crook, William and Laura Stevens. *Solving the Puzzle of Your
Hard-To-Raise Child.* New York: Random House Professional Books, 1987.

Diagnostic and Statistical Manual of Mental Disorders. 4th ed.
Washington, D.C: American Psychiatric Press, 2000.
207-210.

Diamant, M. and B. Diamant. "Abuse and Timing of Use of Antibiotics in Acute Otitis Media." *Archives of Otolaryngology* 100 (September 1974): 226-232.

Donohue, Andrew. "Criticism of RitalinÒ Use Induces Lawsuits,
Federal Investigations." *Bee Washington Bureau,* December 25, 2000.

Egger, J., A. Stolla and L. McEwan. "Controlled Trial of Hyposensitisation in Children with Food-Induced Hyperkinetic Syndrome." *The Lancet* 339 (9 May 1992): 1150-
1153.

Elmer, G. V., C. M. Surawicz, and L. V. McFarland.
"Biotherapeutic Agents: A Neglected Modality for the
Treatment and Prevention of Selected Intestinal and
Vaginal Infections." *Journal of the American Medical
Association* 275 no. II (20 March 1996): 870-876.

"FDA Advisers Tied to Industry." *USA Today Health,* 25 September 2000.

Bibliography

Falth-Magnusson, K., et al. "Gastrointestinal Permeability in Children with Cow's Milk Allergy: Effect of Milk Challenge and Sodium Cromoglycate as Assessed with Polyethyleneglycols (PEG 400 and PEG 1000)." *Clinical Allergy* 16 no. 6 (1986): 543-551.

Frymann, V., R. Carrey, P. Springall. "Effect of Osteopathic Medical Management on Neurological Development in Children." *Journal of the American Osteopathic Association* 92 no. 6 (June 1992): 729-744.

Gillberg, C., H. Melander, A. L. Von Knorring, L. O. Janols, G. Thernlund, B. Hagglof, et al. "Long-term Stimulant Treatment of Children with Attention-Deficit Hyperactivity Disorder Symptoms: A Randomized, Double-Blind, Placebo-Controlled Trial." *Archives of General Psychiatry* 54 (1997): 854-864.

Goldman, J., et al. "Behavioral Effects of Sucrose on Preschool Children." *Journal of Abnormal Child Psychology* 14 no. 4 (1986): 565-577.

"Gunman Kills Girl, Wounds 10 at School." *Los Angeles Times,* 27 September 1988.

Grounds, David, Andrew Stockey, Peter Evans, Colin Scott, Rowan McIntosh, Estelle Morrison, Harry Durham, Rick Yeatman, Peter Farnbach. "Antidepressants and Side Effects." *Australian and New Zealand Journal of Psychiatry* 29 no. 1 (April 1995): 156-157.

Haislip, Gene, Deputy Assistant Administrator, Office of Diversion Control, Drug Enforcement Agency, United States Department of Justice, Washington, D.C., DEA Report, ADD/ADHD Statement of Drug Enforcement Administration, At the conclusion of the Conference on Stimulant Use in the Treatment of ADHD. San Antonio, 10 December-12 1996.

Bibliography

Havel, Peter, and Gerald Taborsky. "The Contribution of the Autonomic Nervous System to Changes of Glucagon and Insulin Secretion during Hypoglycemic Stress." *Endocrine Reviews* 10 no. 1 (1989): 332-350.

Haymond, Morey. "Hypoglycemia in Infants and Children." *Endocrinology and Metabolism Clinics of North America* 18 no. 1 (March 1989): 211-253.

Hofeldt, Fred. "Reactive Hypoglycemia." *Endocrinology and Metabolism Clinics of North America* 18 no. 1 (March 1989): 185-201.

Hoffer, A. "Vitamin B3 Dependent Child." *Schizophrenia* 3 (1971): 107-113.

Jacoby, George and Gordon Archer. "New Mechanisms of Bacterial Resistance to Antimicrobial Agents." *Journal of the American Medical Association* 271 no. 23 (June 15, 1994): 601-612.

Jackson, P.G., et al. "Intestinal Permeability in Patients with Eczema and Food Allergy." *Lancet* 1 no. 8233 (1981): 1285-1286.

Jones A.V., P. McLaughlin, M. Shorthouse, et al. "Food Intolerance: A Major Factor in the Pathogenesis of Irritable Bowel Syndrome." *Lancet* 2 part 2 (20 November 1982): 1115-1117.

Jones, Timothy W. "Enhanced Adrenomedullary Response and Increased Susceptibility to Neuroglycopenia: Mechanisms Underlying the Adverse Effects of Sugar Ingestion in Healthy Children." *Journal of Pediatrics* 1, 126 no. 2 (February 1995): 171-177.

Kaplan, Bonnie, Jane McNicol, et al. "Dietary Replacement in Preschool-Aged Hyperactive Boys." *Pediatrics* 83 no. 1 (January 1989): 7-17.

Bibliography

Katz, K.D., et al. "Intestinal Permeability in Patients with Crohn's Disease and Their Healthy Relatives." *Gastroenterology* 97 no. 4 (1989): 927-931.

Klicka, Christopher J. "Home Schooled Students Excel in College." *Home School Legal Defense Association*, 9 March 2000.

Knoble, M. "2-Dimethylaminoethanol (DMAE) in Behavior Problems of Children." *Science Medicine (Buenos Aires)* 119 (1961): 939-944.

Mahan, Kathleen and Mabel Chase. "Sugar 'Allergy' and Children's Behavior." *Annals of Allergy* 61 (December 1988): 453-458.

Mandel, Boris M. "Foods and Additives Are Common Causes of the Attention Deficit Hyperactivity Disorder in Children." *Annals of Allergy* 72 no. 5 (May 1994): 462-468.

Masand, Prakash, et al. "Suicidal Ideation Related to Fluoxetine Treatment." *The New England Journal of Medicine* 324 no. 6 (7 February 1991).

Mayes, S. D., D. L. Crites, E. O. Bixler, F. J. Humphrey II, R. E. Mattison. "Methylphenidate and ADHD: Influence of Age, IQ and Neurodevelopmental Status." *Developmental Medicine and Child Neurology* 36 (1994): 1099-1107.

Meador, Kimford J. "Cognitive Side-Effects of Antiepileptic Drugs." *Canadian Journal of Neurological Sciences* 21, suppl. 3 (August 12, 1994): S12-S16.

Medical Economics, *Physicians Desk Reference 52d ed.* Medical Economics Company, 1998.

_____, *Physicians Desk Reference 54th ed.* Medical Economics Company, 2000.

Bibliography

_____, *Physicians Desk Reference 55th ed.* Medical Economics Company, 2001.

Moynahan. "Zinc Deficiency and Disturbances of Mood and Visual Behavior." *Lancet* 1 no. 91 (1976).

Muldoon, Kate. "Shooting Spurs Debate on Prozac's Use by Kids." *The Oregonian,* 1 June 1998.

National Institutes of Health Consensus Development Conferences Statement. "Diagnosis and Treatment of Attention Deficit Hyperactivity Disorder (ADHD)." 16 November-18. 1998.

Nsouli, T., M. Nsouli, R. Linde, et al. "Role of Food Allergy in Serious Otitis Media." *Annals of Allergy* 73 no. 3 (September 1994): 215-219.

Oettinger, L. "The Use of DMAE in the Treatment of Disorders of Behavior in Children." *Journal of Pediatrics* 53 (1958): 671-675.

O'Meara, Kelly. "Guns and Doses." *Insight,* 28 June 1999.

Paradis, J. L., Heidi M. Feldman, et al. "Effect of Early or Delayed Insertion of Tympanostomy Tubes for Persistent Otitis Media on Developmental Outcomes at the Age of Three Years." *The New England Journal of Medicine* 344 no. 16 (19 April 2001): 1179-1187.

"Parents Find Clue to Why Their Son Killed." *The Patriot Ledger,* 19 September 1987.

Pfeiffer, C., et al. "Stimulant Effect of 2-Dimethyl-l-aminoethanol (DMAE): Possible Precursor of Brain Acetylcholine." *Science* 126 (1957): 610-611.

Pintal, W. and M. Keutz. "An Integrated Osteopathic Treatment Approach in Acute Otitis Media." *Journal of the American Osteopathic Association* 89 no. 9 (September 1998): 1139-1141.

"Psychiatric Drugs Create Killer." *Freedom,* November/ December 1988.

Rowe, K.S. and K.J. Rowe. "Synthetic Food Coloring and Behavior: A Dose Response Effect in a Double-Blind, Placebo-Controlled, Repeated-Measures Study." *Journal of Pediatrics* 125 no. 5 part 1 (November 1994): 691-698.

Schachlar, R. J., R. Tannock, C. Cunningham, P. V. Corkum. "Behavioral, Situational, and Temporal Effects of Treatment of ADHD with Methylphenidate." *Journal of American Academy of Child and Adolescent Psychiatry* 36 (1997): 754-763.

Schauss, A. G. *Diet, Crime and Delinquency.* Berkeley: Parker House, 1980.

"School Shooting Probe Continues." *The Newton Kansan,* 27 September 1988.

Seelig, Mildred. "Clinical Aspects of Chronic Magnesium Deficiency." *Magnesium in Health and Disease.* New York: Spectrum Press, 1980.

Stanislaus. "The Effect of Nutrition on Crime, Intelligence, Academic Performance, and Brain Function." California State University, 1981-2000.

Teicher, Martin H., et al. "Emergence of Intense Suicidal Preoccupation During Fluoxetine Treatment." *The American Journal of Psychiatry* 147 no. 2 (February 1990).

Bibliography

Toren, et al. "Zinc Deficiency in Attention Deficit Hyperactivity Disorder." *Biological Psychiatry* 40 (1996): 1308-1310.

U.S. Department of Justice, Drug Enforcement Agency, Drug and Chemical Evaluation Section, Office of Diversion Control. "Methylphenidate: A Background Paper."

_____. "Methylphenidate (Ritalin®) Drug and Chemical Evaluation Section," 1995.

U.S. Food and Drug Administration. *Summary of FDA's Adverse Drug Reaction Reports on Prozac*, 1988-1992, obtained through Freedom of Information Act by Citizen's Commission on Human Rights.

Volkow, Nora, Yu-Shein Ding, et al. "Is Methylphenidate Like Cocaine?" *Archives of General Psychiatry* 52 (June 1995): 456-463.

Vuurman, Eric F. P. M., Loe M.A. van Veggel, Mir M. C. Uiterwijk, Detlev Leutner, James F. O'Hanlon. "Seasonal Allergic Rhinitis and Antihistamine Effects on Children's Learning." *Annals of Allergy* 71 (August 1993).

Wagner, R. D., et al. "Biotherapeutic Effects of Probiotic Bacteria on Candidiasis in Immunodeficient Mice." *Infection and Immunity* 65 no. 10 (October 1997): 4165-4172.

Wolraich, Mark. "Intolerance: Is There Evidence For Its Effects on Behavior On Children." *Annals of Allergy* 61 (December 1988): 58-61.

Woodworth, Terrence, Deputy Director, Office of Diversion Control, Drug Enforcement Agency, Drug Enforcement Agency. Congressional Testimony, Committee on Education and the Workforce: Subcommittee on Early Childhood, Youth and Families, 16 May 2000.

Bibliography

Zito, Julie Magno, Daniel J. Safer, Susan dosReis, James F. Gardner, Myde Boles, Frances Lynch. "Trends in the Prescribing of Psychotropic Medications to Preschoolers." *The Journal of the American Medical Association* 283 no. 8 (23 February 2000): 1025.

"15-year-old Sentenced to Life for Killing Classmate with Kicks." *Times Picayune,* 11 March 1988.

Index

Index

N
National Institutes of Health (NIH)... 18, 21, 29, 33, 34, 53
New York... 52, 56, 59, 84, 151, 152
Niacin... 87, 90
No More Antibiotics... 122, 149
No More Ritalin... 149
Norpramine... 23, 44-45
Novartis... 13, 45

O
Optometrist... 133
Osteopathic... 9, 10, 137, 138
Osteopathic Manipulative Treatment (OMT)... 137-145

P
Parenting... 156-157
Paxil... 27, 43-44, 88
Pesticides... *(see Insecticides)*
Physicians' Desk Reference (PDR)... 23, 27, 36, 42-44
Placebo... 63
Probiotics... 118-119
Protein... 70, 72, 89, 99, 121, 131
Prozac... 27, 36-37, 40, 43, 45-46, 88
Psychosis... 4, 39
  psychotic behaviors... 38, 41, 48
  psychotic episode... 38, 42, 43, 44
  psychotic state... 38
  psychotic symptoms... 42

R
Recipes... 75-77
Rice... 70, 100, 109, 111, 121, 126
Right Brain Tactile Learner (RBTL)... 128-134
Ritalin... 45, 135
  abuse of... 28-29, 35, 46
  academic performance and... 53
  allergies compared to... 91
  babies on... 35, 36-37, 45-46
  cocaine compared to... 13, 22-23, 46
  common side effect of... 3-5, 24-25, 34, 42
  diabetes and... 34-35, 74
  DMAE compared to... 88
  education and... 18-19, 51-52, 59, 62
  influences on behavior... 18, 32, 55
  lawsuits... 45, 52-53, 152
  long-term use of... 21-22, 34, 37-38
  manufacturers of... 13
  placebo compared to... 63, 147
  The Road to No More Ritalin... 96
  similar drugs... 39
  use in America... 28